Visions of the Nordic Model in Northern and Southern Europe (1970s–1990s)

Alan Granadino,
Andreas Mørkved Hellenes
& Carl Marklund (eds.)

Södertörns högskola

Institute of Contemporary History
Södertörn University
SE-141 89 Huddinge

shi@sh.se
www.sh.se/shi

Cover: Jonathan Robson
Graphic form: Per Lindblom & Jonathan Robson
Stockholm 2023

Samtidshistoriska frågor nr 45
ISSN: 1650-450X
ISBN: 978-91-89615-45-8

Contents

Introduction

This book is the result of the third in a series of witness seminars that have brought together some of the key political actors associated with a set of historical processes from the 1970s to the 1990s. These processes are: the development of European social democracy during the 1970s; the Northern and Southern processses of European integration, and the fortunes of the so-called Nordic model. The witness seminar format is a variant of oral history that goes beyond the mere exposition of the memories of the historical actors, allowing these actors instead to recall, discuss and debate the historical events among themselves, together with scholarly experts in the field. The overall objective of this seminar series has been to interrogate, listen, record, and transcribe these accounts in the series *Samtidshistoriska frågor* as published by the Institute of Contemporary History at Södertörn University.

The witness seminar "Visions of the Nordic Model in Northern and Southern Europe (1970s-1990s)" focused on the various understandings of the concept of the Nordic model in Northern (specifically Sweden and Denmark) and Southern Europe (specifically Spain) from the 1970s to the 1990s. The aim was to widen our knowledge on the Nordic model and its relationship to Europeanization by analyzing how and in which contexts it was understood, used and conceptualized in these decades. Therefore, we were open to consider the several dimensions of this concept (i.e. a model for foreign policy, a social and economic model, a model for gender equality, a foreign aid model etc.). We consider that the combination of perspectives from Northern and Southern Europe and the contribution of the oral testimonies of our guests (Joaquín Almunia, Allan Larsson and Mogens Lykketoft) are of key importance for producing new knowledge on this topic and for creating a new historical source for future research.

At a first glance, the meaning of the concept of the Nordic model today seems obvious. According to Wikipedia:

> The Nordic model comprises the economic and social policies as well as typical cultural practices common to the Nordic Countries (Denmark, Finland, Iceland, Norway and Sweden). This includes a comprehensive welfare state and multi-level collective bargaining based on the economic foundations of social corporatism, with a high percentage of the workforce unionized and a sizable percentage of the population employed by the public sector.[1]

Another online encyclopedia, such as Investopedia.com, provides a similar definition of this concept:

> The Nordic model is the combination of social welfare and economic systems adopted by Nordic countries. It combines features of capitalism, such as a market economy and economic efficiency, with social benefits, such as state pensions and income distribution. The Nordic model, also known as the Scandinavian model, is most commonly associated with the countries of Scandinavia: Sweden, Norway, Finland, Denmark, and Iceland. The Nordic model embraces both the welfare state and globalization [...].[2]

However, when we look at this concept more closely, we can detect that defining it is not so simple.[3] This concept has been highly contested, both in the past and in the present, inside as well as outside of the Nordic region. As recent examples of this, the centrist Emmanuel Macron in the French presidential elections of 2017 and the leftist Democrat Bernie Sanders in the US presidential primaries of 2016 both used the Nordic model rhetorically, but with quite different meanings. In the Nordic countries, the

---

[1] Wikipedia, "Nordic model." https://en.wikipedia.org/wiki/Nordic_model.
[2] Will Kenton, "Nordic Model: Comparing the Economic System to the U.S," Investopedia. https://www.investopedia.com/terms/n/nordic-model.asp.
[3] Nordics.info, "The Nordic Model." https://nordics.info/themes/the-nordic-model.

Swedish Social Democrats, responding to the attempt of the Conservative and Liberal parties to appropriate the concept, tried to protect their understanding of the model by trademarking it in 2011. In Spain, the populist left-wing party Podemos published its program for the general elections of 2016 in a format that resembled an IKEA catalogue, making an obvious connection between the party and the progressive ideas associated with the Nordic countries. The party also stressed repeatedly that its source of inspiration is the Nordic model, understood in terms of social and economic policy. This sparked public discussion with the Spanish Socialist Workers' Party (PSOE) and with the liberal party Ciudadanos on the meaning of this concept and on who has the right to claim ownership over it. In 2020, moreover, the Swedish response to the Covid-19 pandemic was referred to as the "Swedish model" against Coronavirus and a year later the German broadcaster ZDF talked about the Danish Corona model based on massive testing and a relative open society. In the Nordic countries themselves a debate erupted on whether the Nordic countries' approach is converging on a more or less joint Nordic formula, despite quite different starting points. These examples illustrate the different meanings that the concept of the Nordic model and its variants can contain, but also its diverse application to a variety of phenomena.

The historical narrative on the Nordic model tells us that the Nordic countries have been seen internationally as examples to be followed or to take inspiration from since at least the 1930s. It was from the late 1960s, however, that the Swedish combination of social welfare and economic prowess – referred to as representing a Swedish model – became a widely known concept that served as an avatar for the utopian idea of Nordic success in the political discourses of Europe and beyond. In the context of the Cold War, it ultimately came to be seen as a quintessentially social democratic third way between capitalism and communism that was widely regarded as politically, socially and economically successful. Moreover, the Nordic countries acquired an international reputation due to their engagement in international affairs, promoting political mediation in conflicts and fostering global cooperation.

While the concept of the Swedish model gained currency in the 1960s and 1970s, the term, 'the Nordic model', became more commonly used in the 1980s. However, in the 1990s, an increasing international understanding of the Nordic model as entering a stage of crisis emerged, primarily as a result of economic downturn in Finland and Sweden. After the fall of the Soviet Union and the dissolution of the Eastern bloc in the 1990s, the Swedish/Nordic model understood as a third way between capitalism and communism was questioned also in *Norden*, as both the organization of the welfare state and foreign political positionings came under criticism and were debated in terms of national identity.[4] For example, in 1991 Swedish Conservative Prime Minister Carl Bildt stated that "the time for the Nordic model has passed." Similarly, the Centrist Prime Minister of Finland, Esko Aho, stated in the same year that "the Nordic model is dead."[5] Still, the international debate picked up again in the late 1990s, but this time attention focused on the so-called Danish flexicurity model which also gradually metamorphosed into both a Nordic and a European flexicurity model.[6]

When dealing with a concept such as the Nordic model, it must be noted that in the last decades scholars have called into question a supposed uniformity between Nordic countries. Acknowledging the similarities, they have claimed that the Nordic model is, in

---

[4] A. M. Hellenes, H. A. Ikonomou, C. Marklund & Ada Nissen (eds), "Nordic Nineties," special issue of *Culture Unbound*, Vol. 13, No. 1 (2021).

[5] W. E. Schmidt, "In a Post-Cold War Era, Scandinavia Rethinks itself," *The New York Times*, February 23 1992.
https://www.nytimes.com/1992/02/23/weekinreview/in-a-post-cold-war-era-scandinavia-rethinks-itself.html.

[6] The original two flexicurity model countries were Denmark and the Netherlands, see P. K. Madsen, "'How can it possibly fly?' The Paradox of a Dynamic Labour Market in a Scandinavian Welfare State," in J. L. Campbell, J. A. Hall & O. K. Pedersen (eds), *National Identity and the Varities of Capitalism: The Danish Experience* (Montreal: McGill-Queen's University Press 2006), pp. 321–355; E. Viebrock & J. Clasen, "Flexicurity and welfare reform: A review," *Socio-economic review*, Vol. 7, No. 2 (2009), pp. 305–331.

fact, a model with five exceptions.[7] Historians have pointed out that knowledge related to Nordic exceptionalism is a cultural construction.[8] For the purposes of this witness seminar, it is important to note that this literature set the basis for research on how the Nordic model has been imagined, perceived and conceptualized. Following this line of inquiry, scholars have shown that the Nordic model, and the related notion of a Nordic exceptionalism, has been conceptually constructed through the interplay between national and international images and stereotypes, that this concept has circulated in specific geographical and temporal settings, and that different understandings of it have competed across various social fields.[9]

An interesting example in this sense is that of Spanish politics during the decades analyzed in this seminar. Spain moved from dictatorship to democracy in the mid 1970s. In the following decades the democratic system was consolidated, the country defined its position in the international arena (joining NATO in 1982 and the EEC in 1986) and it developed its hitherto limited welfare state (education, health and the pension system were universalized in the 1980s–1990s). Recent and ongoing research has shown that in these decades there were relevant political, material and cultural transfers between Spain and the Nordic countries.[10] The Spanish socialists claimed that the Swedish/Nor-

---

[7] N. F. Christiansen et al, *The Nordic Model of Welfare. A Historical Reappraisal* (Copenhagen: Museum Tusculanum Press, 2006).

[8] Ø. Sørensen & B. Stråth (eds), *The Cultural Construction of Norden* (Oslo: Scandinavian University Press, 1997).

[9] C. Marklund & K. Petersen, "Return to Sender: American Images of the Nordic Welfare States and Nordic Welfare State Branding," *European Journal of Scandinavian Studies*, Vol. 43, No. 2 (2013), pp. 245–257; K. Musiał, *The Roots of the Scandinavian Model. Images of progress in the Era of Modernisation* (Baden-Baden: Nomos, 2002); H. Byrkjeflot et al. (eds), *The Making and Circulation of Nordic Models, Ideas and Images* (London and New York: Routledge, 2021); B. Rom Jensen, A. M. Hellenes, M. Hilson & C. Marklund, "Modelizing the Nordics: Transdiscursive migrations of Nordic models, c. 1965-2020," *Scandinavian Journal of History* (2022).

[10] A. Granadino & P. Stadius, "Adapting the Swedish Model. PSOE-SAP relations during the Spanish transition to democracy," in H. Byrkjeflot et al.

dic model of welfare was a point of reference for them, and the concept was used in Spanish debates of the 1970s and 1980s on different topics, such as the meaning of social democracy, the reach of welfare provided by the state, gender equality, international policy and Spanish NATO membership. Although little is known about the actual transfer of political and institutional design and practices from the Nordic countries to Spain, political scientists consider that before the economic crisis of 2008, "the Spanish case stood out as the one Mediterranean European country which had gone further in incorporating inputs and traits of the social-democratic Nordic model of welfare capitalism."[11]

The ambition of this seminar was to approach the Nordic model from the perspective provided by Northern and Southern European political actors. This allowed us to explore the transformations and the different understandings of the concept of the Nordic model inside and outside *Norden*. The economic crises of the 1970s and the rise of neoliberalism in the 1980s posed a challenge to the Nordic model in economic terms, but it was after the end of the Cold War that the political, social, economic and international dimensions of the Nordic model were fundamentally challenged – and renegotiated not least in the light of prospective European Union membership. Recent research has shown that Nordic initiatives and the collaboration between social democrats from Northern and Southern Europe and members of the European Commission were relevant for the concretization of the employment title inserted into the 1997 Amsterdam Treaty of the EU.[12] Moreover, it seems that the ensuing discussions around the continent over the future of a social Europe as a "European

---

(eds), *The Making and Circulation of Nordic Models, Ideas and Images* (London and New York: Routledge, 2021), pp. 102–123.

[11] L. Moreno, "The Nordic Path of Spain's Mediterranean Welfare," Center for European Studies Working Paper Series, No. 163 (2008).

[12] M. Fulla, "Put (Southern) Europe to Work. The Nordic Turn of European Socialists in the early 1990s," in A. Granadino, S. Nygård & P. Stadius (eds), *Rethinking European Social Democracy and Socialism. The History of the Centre-Left in Northern and Southern Europe in the Late 20th Century* (London and New York: Routledge, 2022), pp. 48–66.

social model" sparked renewed interest in the past and present of the Nordic model(s) into the new millennium.[13] Considering that the external images of the Nordic model and its internal visions are interdependent and mutually constitutive, we consider it valuable to investigate how this concept was perceived, used and transformed in Northern and Southern Europe during this period.

We have focused specifically on Spain, where the Nordic model became a myth and a rhetorical device for the socialists, who were in charge of consolidating democracy, redefining Spain's international policy and building the welfare state in the 1980s. We also wish to shed new light on how and if notions of a Nordic social model were brought into the European level following the adhesions of Sweden and Finland, as well as the sites and arenas where such encounters took place. Through combining the Southern and Northern European perspectives we will explore the different timelines and multilevel development and the meanings of this concept in *Norden* and abroad.

The topic discussed here, and the chronology chosen are quite broad. Our intention was to ignite debate and conversation among the speakers, whose subjective experiences are valuable in themselves and, also, for opening new perspectives that could inform further research and reflection on the Nordic model.

Alan Granadino, Complutense University of Madrid
Andreas Mørkved Hellenes, Chalmers University of Technology
Carl Marklund, Södertörn University

---

[13] B. Rom Jensen, A. M. Hellenes, M. Hilson & C. Marklund, "Modelizing the Nordics: Transdiscursive migrations of Nordic models, c. 1965–2020," *Scandinavian Journal of History* (2022).

Participants

Researchers

Alan Granadino, Postdoctoral researcher, Complutense University of Madrid

Andreas Mørkved Hellenes, Researcher, Chalmers University of Technology

Mary Hilson, Professor, Aarhus University

Peter Stadius, Professor, University of Helsinki

Thorsten Borring Olesen, Professor, Aarhus University

Witnesses

Allan Larsson, Journalist, trade unionist and social democratic politician who has served as Swedish Finance Minister, Member of the Swedish Parliament and Director General in the EU Commission. He has also served as special adviser to President Juncker on the European Pillar of Social Right and as vice chair on EU Mission Board on Climate Neutral Cities.

Mogens Lykketoft, Social democrat politician who served as Danish Minister of Taxation between 1980 and 1981. He was Minister of Finance from 1993 to 2000 and Minister of Foreign Affairs from 2000 to 2001. After that he was leader of the Social Democrats between 2002 and 2005, Speaker of the Parliament of Denmark from 2011 to 2015 and President of the United Nations General Assembly from 2015 to 2016.

Joaquín Almunia, Socialist politician. He was the chief economist of the socialist trade union UGT from 1976 to 1979. He served as Spanish Minister of Employment and Social Security from 1982 to 1986, and as Minister of Public Administration from 1986 to 1991. After that he was European Commissioner for Economic and Financial Affairs (2004–2010) and for Competition (2010–2014). He has been Member of the Spanish Parliament from 1979 to 2004, and leader of PSOE from 1997 to 2000.

Abbreviations

CFDT	Confédération française démocratique du travail
CIOSL	Confederación Internacional de Organizaciones Sindicales Libres
DGB	Deutscher Gewerkschaftsbund
EFTA	European Free Trade Association
EMU	The European and Monetary Union
EU	European Union
GDP	Gross Domestic Product
IMF	International Monetary Fund
NATO	North Atlantic Treaty Organization
OECD	Organisation for Economic Co-operation and Development
PSOE	Partido Socialista Obrero Espanol
PvdA	Partij van de Arbeid
SFIO	Section française de l'Internationale ouvrière
SPD	Sozialdemokratische Partei Deutschlands
TUC	Trade Union's Congress
UGT	Unión General de Trabajadores
US	United States

Witness Seminar

Mary Hilson

Good afternoon everybody! Welcome very much to this witness seminar with three distinguished guests. My colleague Peter Stadius is going to formally welcome you and say something about this seminar. Before we start though, I just wanted to say a few short things about the technicalities this afternoon.

My name is Mary Hilson and I am professor of history here at Aarhus University. First thing, you should already be aware of when you signed up, that the seminar will be recorded and transcribed. So, I have started the recording. The intention is to produce a publication for the series *Samtidshistoriska frågor* published by Södertörns högskola in Sweden. So, it will be recorded. With the exception of the speakers, I would also like to ask if all guests could kindly keep their microphones and their cameras off at all times during the seminar.

There will be an opportunity for audience questions later on, and if you are asking questions at that point, then you may turn on your camera and your microphone. And then thirdly, as I said, there will be an opportunity for questions, but questions will be moderated. So, if you would like to ask a question, please can you write in the chat as a private message to myself. And we would like to ask you not to use the chat for general messages to the whole seminar, because we think it is a little bit distracting if there are messages pinging in and out all the time. And please remember anyway that the chat messages are in any case part of the recording. There will be two short breaks during the seminar, lasting for around 15 minutes each. We would recommend you do not log off during the break, but if you lose the connection, do not worry: we will readmit you afterwards. Without any further ado, then, I will hand over to Peter Stadius who will say something about the seminar.

Peter Stadius

Thank you so much, Mary. For my part as well, welcome everybody to this witness seminar. I am Peter Stadius, professor of Nordic Studies at the University of Helsinki. And this is a joint cooperation between Aarhus University, Södertörn University and the University of Helsinki. It is part of a project called "Contemporary Europe Told from its Nordic and Southern Perspectives," funded by the NOS-HS Fund for Social Science and Humanities by the NordForsk Joint Nordic Funding Institution. We have arranged one witness seminar already and the publication is on the way.

This is the second witness seminar in this series. And we have three very experienced politicians as our speakers today. They all share many things concerning European politics. Joaquín Almunia has served both as a cabinet member and a party leader for the Spanish Socialist Party [PSOE], and then later in this millennium as a commissioner, a member of the EU Commission. Of course, we could go on at length mentioning many other things, also as a teacher and professor of practice, that Joaquín Almunia has in his curriculum, but I just want to express my deep gratitude that we are able to assemble such an illustrious and interesting group. It also gives me a lot of pleasure to have this North and South comparison and dialogue. Mogens Lykketoft, also a former minister and party leader of the Danish Social Democratic Party as well, extremely experienced, and together with the other participants, a specialist in economic politics and finance, but also social policy and social questions. Allan Larsson, also Minister of Finance in the early 1990s in the Swedish government, and a civil servant with a vast array of expert assignments both nationally and on the European and international levels. All three of you have seen from the inside the development from the 1980s onwards of the European integration and all the political questions that arise therefrom. So, for my part, welcome to the speakers; I really enjoy your participation.

Two words on this witness seminar concept. It is a concept developed by Södertörn University and the Institute for Contemporary History – and I see also that Norbert Götz[1] is present here among the audience. The idea is to have politicians or other actors, who have been part of important, contemporary historical events, to meet up, and remember, give their versions and analyze. This is then transcribed into a publication. The witness seminar publication series has I don't know how many volumes,[2] maybe Norbert could answer that better. But that is the idea behind this: that researchers, academic scholars meet up with the actors of remarkable important events in our recent, contemporary history. So, for my part welcome everybody to this seminar.

Mary Hilson
Thank you, Peter. Now I give the way to Andreas. He is going to say something, a little bit about the Nordic model concept just to start this up.

Andreas Mørkved Hellenes
Thank you very much, Mary. To those who do not know me, my name is Andreas Mørkved Hellenes, I am a historian working at Chalmers University of Technology in Gothenburg currently. Before we turn to the witnesses and today's conversation, I thought that I would just say a few words about why we as contemporary historians are interested in this topic, namely the border-crossing history of ideas, or notions, about the Nordic model, as well as certain policies or institutional experiences developed in the Nordic region.

Together with colleagues at Aarhus, I have in the last few years been working on the research project "Nordic Models in the Global Circulation of Ideas, 1970s to 2020s." A project, I should

---

[1] Professor Norbert Götz at the Institute for Contemporary History at Södertörn University.

[2] At the time of this witness seminar, this series had published 42 volumes.

mention, led by Mary Hilson, where we try to study precisely such phenomena in various ways. We have approached the research topic of the Nordic model from various angles: we have for example investigated the conceptual history of the concept of the Nordic model – when people started talking about it, which meanings they attributed to it, how the concept moved across borders and cultures through processes of translation between languages etcetera. We have also mapped out the usages of the concept of the Nordic model in international scientific literature, in order to examine the dynamics between politics and social science. We have looked at the political usages of the concept outside of the Nordic region to seek to better understand the rhetorical function that Norden and the Nordic model has performed in both present and past debates about the future of the welfare state.

To put it short, or so I would dare to suggest, we have established that the Nordic model is and has always been a transnational concept. Yet, it remains a fact that most of the research that historians have done focus on the English speaking world. Taken into joint consideration the international prominence of the United States in the last century and its political and cultural impact in the Nordic countries, notably during the Cold War, it is hardly surprising that the transatlantic dimension continues to attract and fascinate researchers. It is the ambition of this seminar, however, to relocate focus to the European stage in order to, hopefully, shed new light on other links and connections between the Nordic countries and the outside world than the quite well-researched Nordic-American relations.

Such a shift in focus from the Atlantic towards the Continental European is obviously motivated by temporal considerations as well. As the 1980s and 1990s are opened up for historical research, new questions arise about the Nordic countries' relationship with both individual European countries and the process of European integration. In a moment where it is impossible to ignore not only the renewed importance of the Atlantic Alliance with questions about membership in Finland and Sweden, but also of the European project, not least in a Northern European perspective, it seems highly relevant to revisit the European dimension of the history of the Nordic model.

Alan Granadino

Thank you very much, Andreas. And for those of you who do not know me, my name is Alan Granadino, I am one of the co-organizers of this witness seminar. I am also a historian and I am currently a post-doctoral researcher at the Complutense University of Madrid.

In the light of what Andreas just has said, an interesting example is that of the Iberian Peninsula. Following this trend of research in the transnational dimension of the Nordic model, tracing connections, exchanges and transfers between Norden and other parts of Europe has been interesting. For instance, in the last years, researchers have shown that there have been relevant transnational connections between Nordic and Iberian political actors between the 1970s and 1990s. As far as we know, this work was predominantly promoted and facilitated by social democratic actors and networks.

For example, recent research by Carl Marklund [and Jan Olsson],[3] which is still to be published if I am not wrong, shows that the Swedish social democrats encouraged the development of a democratic society in Portugal in the 1970s and the 1980s, through support given to the Portuguese Socialist Party on the one hand, and to the cooperative movement in Portugal on the other hand, through what was called the Portugal campaign.

In the case of Spain, the country went from dictatorship to democracy in the mid-1970s, and in the following decades the democratic system was consolidated, the country defined its position in the international arena – joining NATO in 1982 and the European Economic Community in 1986 – and it developed its hitherto limited welfare state. Recent and ongoing research shows

---

[3] C. Marklund & J. Olsson, "The Portugal campaign: Swedish cooperative assistance in Portugal after the Carnation Revolution." Paper presented at "Nordic models in global entanglements: Towards a contemporary global history of the Nordic region." Workshop at Comwell Kolding 11–12 November 2021.

that in these decades there were relevant political, material and cultural transfers between Spain and the Nordic countries, especially Sweden. The Spanish socialists claimed that the Swedish/Nordic model of welfare was a point of reference for them. And the concept was used in Spanish political debates in the 1970s and the 1980s on different topics, such as what the meaning of social democracy was; the reach and characteristics of welfare provided by the state; gender equality; and even international policy and Spanish NATO membership.

These reflect the various meanings attached to this concept and its polyvalence. But it also suggests that it is a concept open to contestation. Although little is known about the actual transfer or emulation of political and institutional design and practices from the Nordic countries to Spain, political scientists such as Luis Moreno consider that before the economic crisis of 2008, and I quote, "the Spanish case stands out as the one Mediterranean European country, which had gone farther in incorporating inputs and trades of the social democratic Nordic model of welfare capitalism."[4] End of quote.

So, the ambition of this seminar is to approach the Nordic model from the ample perspectives provided by Northern and Southern European political actors. This will allow us to explore the transformations and the different understandings of the concept of the Nordic model inside and outside of Norden. Considering that the external images of the Nordic model and its internal visions are interdependent and mutually constitutive, we consider valuable to investigate how this concept was perceived, used and transformed in Northern and Southern Europe during this period. Moreover, we wish to shed new light on how and if notions of the Nordic social model were brought into the European level following the adhesions of Sweden and Finland.

By combining the Northern and Southern European perspectives, we will explore the different timelines in the multi-level development, and the meanings of this concept in Norden and

---

[4] L. Moreno, L., "The Nordic Path of Spain's Mediterranean Welfare", Center for European Studies Working Paper Series, No. 163 (2008), p. 1.

abroad. So, the topic discussed here is quite broad and the chronology chosen is also quite broad, so our intention is to ignite debate and conversation among the speakers, whose experiences will be valuable in themselves and, also, for opening new perspectives that could inform further research and reflection on the Nordic model. Thank you very much for being here, and now without further ado I give the floor to Mary Hilson who will start with the questions.

Mary Hilson

Thanks very much, Alan and Andreas, for starting us off. So, I would now like to go to our three guests and to start the conversation. Perhaps just to get us started, could I ask the three of you just briefly to tell us a little bit more about your political roles and your positions during the period we were talking about, the 1980s and 1990s, just by way of introduction. So perhaps, Allan, we could start with you?

Allan Larsson

Thank you for inviting me. It is a great pleasure to be here, to meet old friends, and to discuss a very interesting topic. I myself worked in the 1970s in the trade union movement as a chief economist for the metal workers, then I became Undersecretary of labour, and in the 80s I was Director-General for the national labour market administration. In the 90s I became Minister of Finance and a member of parliament, and then I became Director-General in the EU Commission, in DG Employment and Social Affairs. So that is my brief story of what I did during these three decades.

Mary Hilson

Thank you very much. Mogens Lykketoft, can we ask you to say something?

Mogens Lykketoft

Yes. I have been engaged in Social Democratic Movement politics for more than 40 years. I started as a student leader in the 60s. I worked with the Economic Board of the Danish labour movement for some years, before I was appointed Minister of Taxation in the early 80s. Then we had a long period, which is really a very interesting topic for discussion today, of Centre-Right government. For ten years I was elected to parliament, was in opposition, as the spokesman for taxation and economic policy. I rejoined as Minister for Finance for nearly eight years from 1993, where we did some basic reforms of the Nordic model in Denmark and were successful in turning a very high unemployment – 350 000, 12%, in the beginning of our term – to much, much less and a surplus in the economy in the end of the 1990s. That has been my role in the economic policy. Later on I was Foreign Minister and party chairman for a while and joined the United Nations as President of the General Assembly.

Mary Hilson

Thank you very much. And then Joaquín Almunia, can I also ask you please, to say briefly something about your role and your political positions.

Joaquín Almunia

Yes of course. Thank you very much for inviting me to this extremely interesting discussion. I became the Chief Economist of the Labour Union – the *Unión General de Trabajadores*, UGT – that is oriented closely with the Socialist Party platforms. This was a moment when the Union, immediately after Franco's death, was ready to open an office in Madrid – the first time since the Civil War.[5] It was not legally accepted. We were not yet legal, but we were accepted, because after Franco's death the government was not able to put pressure on this kind of democratic movement. So, I spent three years there as the Chief Economist of the Union. At the beginning I was the only one, so I was the Chief of myself. In 1979, three years after, I was elected in Parliament, on the Socialist Party list. And in 1982, in October, we won the elections and I was Minister of Labour and Social Security during the first govern-

---

[5] The Spanish Civil War (1936–1939).

ment of Felipe González.[6] And three and a half years after, in 1986, I moved my portfolio toward public administration issues. I was elected leader of the party after Felipe González's resignation in 1997, and I lost the elections in 2000 and resigned as the leader of the party. I remained in the Parliament, and in 2004 after the Zapatero[7] election as a new Socialist Prime Minister, I was proposed by him as a member of the European Commission. And I spent three and a half years as a member of the European Commission. First, in charge of the Economic Affairs portfolio, and in 2010 until the end of 2014, Commissioner for Competition.

Mary Hilson

Thank you very much. So, I think the first thing I would like to ask all three of you – with your very distinguished careers behind you and really being at the centre of politics, not only nationally, but also internationally – is about this Nordic model concept, which is our focus today. How do you understand it? Because I think we as scholars think we have a certain way of thinking about it, but what does it mean to you? And Allan Larsson perhaps we can start with you?

Allan Larsson

Let me begin with a story that goes back to the end of the 60s. That time I did not know about a "Swedish model." I had not heard the word before. And suddenly it appeared in a book, written by a French journalist, Jean-Jacques Servan-Schreiber, editor-in-chief of *L'Express*. He wrote the book *Le défi américain*, published in 1967.[8] He had a chapter, a final chapter, in that book, called "The Swedish model": "Le modèle suédois." It was the first time I ever heard about the model. And we were flattered, but on the other hand we realized that you cannot have a model and sell it to others, because institutions are so different, traditions are so dif-

---

[6] Felipe González was Prime Minister of Spain from 1982 to 1996.

[7] José Luis Rodriguez Zapatero was Prime Minister of Spain from 2004 to 2011.

[8] Jean-Jacques Servan-Schreiber, founder and editor of the weekly news magazine *L'Express*, was an influential press voice in France and beyond. His book *Le défi américain* (Eng. *The American Challenge*) was a global best-seller.

ferent, cultures are different. And, therefore, you have to have a lot of respect for others. So, while we were pleased to see such a nice chapter about our policies, we realized that this is not what we can go out and say, that you should copy us. It is not possible. If you now accept the phrase "model" – Swedish or Nordic model – I think that basically it is about a new balance between economic and social aspects, social forces. Bringing the working people, through trade union engagement, closer into the centre ground of economic policy. That is, I would say, the basic meaning with it; it takes many, many different ways, but that is in my way the core. Let us start with that and see if Mogens and Joaquín have a similar, or different, take on this.

Mary Hilson

I think that is a very good place to start. And I'll maybe come back to you about, the Swedish or Nordic – you said yourself Swedish or Nordic model – but let us leave that for the moment. And Mogens Lykketoft I would like to ask you, do you agree with this? Is that also how you understand this Nordic model term? But, also, I suppose from you looking more at the Danish model perspective.

Mogens Lykketoft

I agree with what Allan said about the impossibility of just exporting a national model or the Nordic model, because it has some specific historical and institutional background going far back in the past. And even if you compare the Nordic models, there are pretty many institutional differences. They all add up to be characterized by a long period of Social Democratic government dominating most of the 20th century. Some in their own majority, some in coalition with other parties, but anyway characterized with the Social Democratic dominance in government and very strong trade unions, working together, having a kind of division of labour, where we could lift living conditions for ordinary people, sometimes through trade union activities, sometimes through parliament legislation and include more people than we had been able to do through the trade unions. That is kind of characteristic. And then the fact that in the Nordic countries you have less inequality in distribution of wealth and income than in most other parts of the world because of, traditionally, a high level of taxation, a progressive level of taxation and using most of the money for social profits: social care; old age care; education; children; families, and so on. So, you pay according to your ability and you get according to your needs, so to say. And that adds up to a much more equal distribution of disposable income than in most other places. I think that is the common denominator of the Nordic model. But there are very big differences in the way we have been doing it.

Mary Hilson

Thank you. You have both of you seen it from within, as it were, from respected positions in Sweden and Denmark. Can both of you, before we come to Joaquín Almunia, can you both comment a bit on the ways in which you understand the Nordic vis à vis the Danish or the Swedish model? Because Allan Larsson you started off very much talking about a Swedish model, but then you said Swedish or Nordic.

Allan Larsson

If I can start, I would say that the common idea in the Nordic countries, as Social Democratic Parties were in government in the 1940s and 1950s – and saved very much the politics in the period after the war – at that time there was a choice to be made between a Continental model, the Bismarck model, with pensions and social rights linked to your work, and the Beveridge model, the Labour model for the UK, which linked pensions and social benefits to citizenship. So, should you address citizens, or should you address workers with your policies? That was the choice at that time. But I think that all the Scandinavian countries did a third choice: that was to take both social rights related to citizenship and social rights related to income from work. I think this is the main element of the Nordic model. Or what do you say Mogens?

Mogens Lykketoft

I think you are very much right, and especially when you look at the pension schemes, this combination is very strong, in Denmark at least. I think we have some of the most well-funded, well-organized combinations of public pension for everybody and increasing labour market pension schemes, which is very sustainable: I think most other European countries have problems with the sustainability of the funding of the pension schemes, because of the changing demographic, increasing elderly population and so on.

If you ask about differences between, for instance, Sweden and Denmark, I think the most important difference historically has been that Sweden had a strong public production sector also. You were much more involved in business from the side of the state in the early period after World War Two. We never had that: we did not have the big companies, we did not have the mines, we did not have steel works and so on. It was smaller, medium sized companies most of them – some big ones operating at sea and in shipping and so on, but mostly smaller, medium sized companies. So maybe you can say that Denmark historically had, in the business policy, a more liberal model, a more privatized model, than Sweden, and Norway I think also. But we combined it with this high level of social protection and taxation.

Mary Hilson

So, similarities in the sense of progressive taxation, public sector in the welfare state, but structural differences in the economy. But did you actually use the terms Nordic or Swedish/Danish model? Does that actually matter to you and how you thought of these policies? Allan, you already mentioned *Le défi américain* from the late 1960s, which explicitly talks about a Swedish model, but did you think in those terms? Were you talking about a Swedish model or a Nordic model?

Allan Larsson

I can say that at that time I, and I think most other Swedish politicians, we did not think in these terms of a model. We were developing something, and we were comparing, not least on the Nordic level: the party leaders – they were Prime Ministers – and they met regularly and people around them did it too. So, we inspired each other, and we learned from each other, but we had a different source of solution. So, we were not too much occupied with a certain model, because if you think it is a model, that is something very strict, but this was more a process or a set of policy innovations, that we saw. When I started to realize, besides this Servan-Schreiber chapter, it was when we became a member of the European Union in 1995, and the three Nordic countries Finland, Denmark and Sweden, popped up in Eurostat statistics, in social, economic, environmental and other areas: we performed well in these areas. And that gave a sort of focus on "what are they doing, these Nordic countries?"

Mary Hilson

That is very interesting, because I think there has been a lot of focus recently on these indexes and international measurements of happiness, wellbeing, all sorts of things. But you actually say, that there is also a turning point in 1995, that the European measurements of this could actually make a difference.

Mogens Lykketoft

I think that there are two kinds of answers. I was very much aware, when I joined the Social Democratic Movement in 1964, that in this part of the world – Denmark, Norway, Sweden – we had created, up till then, most harmonious, most socially right, kind of society, and that was worth fighting for. But we did not use the model term at that time. That was, as Allan just explained, much later. But the international interest around the Nordic model – at least what I experienced with the Danish model – was that it was impossible for most neoliberal economists and politicians to understand how the Danish bumblebee could fly this very, very heavy level of taxation – and even become one of the most competitive economies in the global scene. This about happiness, competitiveness, rather more fair distribution than in most other countries, and ranking very high also in the transparency international index: there is a connection here, there is a connection here with happiness, transparency, social justice and that was the wonder on the neoliberal side: that we had become the most competitive societies in the world. Because we used the money from the high taxes for education, for social inclusion, used our human resources better, also those who came from poor conditions, and so on. That is really the explanation. And in later times also this surprise, that we were able, at a much higher speed, to integrate IT in our public sector and business, and that has contributed to the continued competitiveness of Danish society.

Allan Larsson

Can I add one thing to that about your phrase "how can the bumblebee fly"? It was a well-known economist from Harvard who made a study for a Swedish institute on this in the end of the 80s, at a time when the tax level was highest in Sweden and the second highest in Denmark. How can the bumblebee fly? And his explanation was that the systems are designed to promote employment, by active labour market policies, by trade union activities, by childcare provisions, and so on. All these systems are there to support people to go into work and to stay there. So that is the explanation. And I think that you Mogens, you did a wonderful job during your periods as Finance Minister, when you step by step changed the Danish system to become more employment oriented than it was before.

Mogens Lykketoft

Yes, I think what we really did in the beginning of the 90s – when starting with this very high unemployment we were left with at the end of a government that expected unemployment to disappear through market forces at some point – what we did was actually to realize that with the very high rate of change in the labour market, in the job positions, an actual labour market policy had to be much stronger than it used to be, in order to give people out of work the capacity, the qualifications, the support to get another kind of job, because the economy was no longer that you had ups and downs and many people returned to the same facility, the same business, where they used to work. There was a total change: jobs were disappearing from the production sector out of Nordic countries, out of Europe, to Asia – and we had to live from other kind of activities and we had to equip our people to be able to do that. And that was what we actually did successfully in the 1990s.

Mary Hilson

Then there are two big changes. And one of which, I think Allan, you mentioned about joining the European Union and the visibility of the Nordic countries in the statistics, and then Mogens as you mentioned this structural transition with a recession in the early 1990s. I would like to bring Joaquín Almunia in now, and to ask you with a perspective from outside the Nordic region: how did you understand the Nordic model? What did it represent? Where did you come across it? What is your thinking about it?

Joaquín Almunia

The understanding of what we call not the Nordic, but Scandinavian model, is of course very similar to the definitions given by Allan and Mogens: strong unions with close relations with Social Democratic Parties, occupying, those parties, a very prominent position in the political system – not always in government, but for long periods in government. And close relations between the parties and the unions, given the fact that, at least from the first two or three decades, to the left of the Social Democratic Parties there were no strong competitors, and that the unions have unified confederations, whereas our country and in Southern European countries, there were at that time strong Communist Parties, communist oriented unions, and the relationship between parties and unions was not as close as it was seen at least from the Southern Europe.

There were, as Allan Larsson said, in the Scandinavian countries very, very high levels of employment rates, because of the female incorporation into the labour market. That was a position very different from ours. These high employment rates allowed this very good combination of our view of the Nordic model between economic efficiency and competitiveness on the one hand, and capacity to collect taxes – you have very high levels of tax to GDP ratios, and this allowed the funding of powerful welfare states. Welfare states that of course were based on the so called three pillars of the traditional welfare states: pensions, health services, education, but also in the case of the Scandinavian model, childcare, disabled people care, elderly care, that helped at the same time to increase the employment rates and to protect in a very efficient way the rights of the weakest members of our societies.

I think this was our vision of the Nordic model or the Scandinavian model. I can complement this, in particular in the case of Sweden, that I know best: a very good treatment of migrants or exiled people from for instance Latin American countries or other countries. And, it was very, very attractive from our point of view in our own country: the high concept of the need of international solidarity. If you are a Social Democrat, you support a strong social welfare state, and you do not forget the foreigners – neither within your country, immigrants or exile people, nor outside, beyond your borders, the international cooperation.

We benefitted from this international support, international solidarity, when we were not a democracy, until the end of 1975, and after, we were inspired by the foreign cooperation for developing countries and for the weakest parts of our world by the actions carried out by the Scandinavian countries. This is my definition. Of course, another thing is to what extent a country such as Spain, in the south of Europe, with a much weaker economy, with its structural problems, can translate, in a short period of time, this model to our country. This is another issue.

Mary Hilson
That issue, though, is quite interesting, because did you see this as directly relevant? Were there specific policies, were there specific

areas where you thought there were things you could learn, transfer?

Joaquín Almunia

Yes. Of course, we try to be inspired by the Nordic countries' experiences, but it was not always easy. For instance, Allan Larsson mentioned active labour market policies. In a country such as Spain, with a very, very high level of unemployment and lower rates of employment: for us, it was absolutely needed to have well organized active labour market policies.

I remember, when I was Labour Minister at the beginning of my mandate, one of my first visits outside of Spain was to Stockholm to meet my colleague, the Labour Minister of Sweden Anna-Greta Leijon, and she explained to me, she and her team explained, active labour market policies. I was of course impressed but coming back to Spain with unemployment going up very quickly, with very weak employment services, with different traditions of labour market negotiations, it was not possible to translate, in a short period of time, these practices. Or, in the case of female employment: yes, we tried to be inspired by the systems that the so-called, the fourth pillar of the welfare state – I follow Gøsta Esping-Andersen's analysis of the welfare states in Europe,[9] three categories, and for us this experience was inspiring, of course.

We managed to organize such services. We had some very good experiences and results, but of course without the public resources coming from taxation at a similar level or close to the levels of the Scandinavian countries. The Spanish system, in other southern countries in Europe also, is not possible to advance very quickly toward the implementation of those services. So, we had economic limits regarding how we could translate the good inspirations and the good examples of the Nordic model in weaker economies, and with different traditions on top of this.

---

[9] Almunia is referring to Gøsta Esping-Andersen's book *The Three Worlds of Welfare Capitalism* (1990).

Mary Hilson

I would like to ask a question to all three of you, which is – we are talking about models and in this case the Scandinavian, Nordic or Swedish, Danish models. But of course they are also models in a world of other models, and all countries, all political parties, organizations learning from each other, and transnational policy transfer is part of that – so, putting this Nordic model idea in a broader context: what other ideas, what other transnationalities, transnational sharing of policy and politics informed the debates you were having about welfare state, labour market and so forth?

Joaquín Almunia

I can mention one clear example in Spain: the British National Health Service. This is funded on Beveridge's ideas. And Allan Larsson mentioned before the Beveridge model. And we in Spain copied the basis of the British National Health Service, because our pension system comes from the Bismarck origin, it is a pay as you go based on those who work or that wants to work or are unemployed, but in any case, the pension system is based on and funded by social contributions of the employees and employers, and the health service instead was funded progressively, and now 100 percent by taxes. So, the health service is a service for citizens, but the pension system is a pension for workers or for people that worked or for people that wants to work or whatever. As well as the unemployment protection system, also based on social contributions, so we pick up inspirations from both big models of welfare state: the Bismarck and the British model. The Swedish and the Scandinavians did the same, but with much more resources and with much better experiences on how to implement this mixed model, that was defined in the previous interventions.

Mary Hilson

Indeed, and Allan, you already mentioned this, but thinking more specifically about the context of the 1980s and early 1990s. Are there other factors: what are the transnational policy models and ideas, circulating at that point? And in the Nordic countries, is it about transfers within the region, Denmark, Sweden, SAMAK[10] and so forth, or a broader European context?

Allan Larsson

Could you please give me the question a bit more precise?

Mary Hilson

Yeah, I'm sorry. Joaquín explained Beveridge and Bismarck models, which you had also mentioned, in the 1940s and 1950s. But if we are a bit more specific coming to the 1980s and 1990s, what other examples of policy transfer and model exchanges were there?

Allan Larsson

I think that we continued in some way the basic development of the policies, of this combination of policies, for example, fiscal policy, active labour market policy and the wages policy of solidarity. It was a way to bring low-paid workers up to better standards. That was the basic combination in Swedish economic policy: restricted fiscal policy, very active labour market policy, and a wages policy that gave more to those who are least paid.

So that was the basic idea, but then in the 80s and 90s there came a new, should I say international, wave. And I think in terms of the long political waves. This is a concept, Kondratiev's concept.[11] And in my lifetime I have experienced two such long waves. One from the mid-40s to the mid-70s-early 80s. And that was the rebuilding of Europe, the rebuilding of the institutions, the building of European integration, and so on. And the building of welfare societies, based on Keynes' ideas. That was the first long wave. It was an extremely successful long wave. And then in the 70s, we came into a situation, where the international economic order did not work: we had the Vietnam War – the United States borrowed to fight the war – where the oil price shocked us all. And then we

---

[10] SAMAK is the Cooperation Committee of the Nordic Labour Movement.

[11] Allan Larson here refers to Nikolai Kondratiev, a Soviet economist who was one of the promotors of the New Economic Policy in the Soviet Union. Kondratiev observed cycles in the world economy in his book *The Major Economic Cycles* published in 1925.

had stagflation – high inflation and stagnation in economic terms. And then people started to say that Keynes' ideas do not give us any answers for this situation, so we had to find something new. And then the Chicago School and the international institutions like IMF and others, they came with a new neoliberal concept, which has been the long wave since the 80s.

So, we have lived through this period and it worked until 2008, when the whole idea of the concept imploded. So, we did not get more growth, but had slower growth; we did not get more stability, we had instability; we did not get equal shares or equality, we had greater economic differences in our societies. These were the two long waves. And that has had a huge impact on the way we can run this form of social economic policies, which we are talking about as Scandinavian, Nordic models. I think that there is a choice, even when there is a long wave of this sort: you can either be to the right or you can be to the left. That is a big difference, even if the main direction is in globalization, more market-oriented economic policies and so on. So, I think that there is always a choice to do. And I think we have tried to do that. Sometimes with success, not always with success.

Mogens Lykketoft
In Denmark, we had an extraordinarily long period of Centre-Right coalitions governing from 1982 to 1993. They were of course somewhat influenced by the neoliberal way of Reagan[12] and Thatcher[13] – liberalization of capital movements, less progressive taxation and so on – but not extremely strong changes, because they thought that social democratic thinking was so strong that they would lose if they fulfilled all the ambitions of change in the direction of the Chicago School, I think. But what they illustrated, was this belief that government was more a problem than a solution

---

[12] Ronald Reagan was President of the United States of America from 1981 to 1989.

[13] Margaret Thatcher was Prime Minister of the United Kingdom from 1979 to 1990.

and that is why they did not intervene in the strong increase in unemployment in the late 1980s.

When we came back, for eight years from 1993, when I was the Minister for Finance, we somewhat felt that we worked against the international tide in economic thinking in actually supporting the creation of jobs, neo-Keynesian policies, and we also illustrated that it was possible to do it – even within one country in an open European economy, because what was learned from that exercise was that Denmark came out better than those who followed more strictly the new tide of neoliberal economic policy.

But your question was, how did we get inspiration over time. We took a lot of inspiration back in time from Swedish active labour market policy, and we implemented it later, maybe, to a full scale, but we did that in 1990s. We got a lot of inspiration from conversations and small working groups' cooperation within what is called SAMAK, between the Nordic Social Democratic Parties and the trade unions.

I took part in some of that work during the 1980s, where we tried to find our way in the new environment and, also, how to modernize our public sector. So that was the main inspiration, but I think the roots of the Nordic model was back in the 1930s, when you had the first strong social democratic goverments fighting against the Global Depression. But the second wave you can characterize as creating the framework for women's participation in the economy.

That is what happened from the late 1950s onwards, providing childcare and so on and so forth, and creating a lot of care jobs, so to say, for ill people, for old people and for children, in the public sector, and in that way also promoting women's participation in the labour market. That created the new, broader public institutions and the service sector, and the need also for a much higher level of taxation. We did that somewhat differently, but I think the trend was exactly the same in the Nordic countries.

Mary Hilson

Thank you. I would like to move on to talk about social democracy, socialism and, actually, we also have a question from Monica Quirico about that. But I would like to suggest that we have a short break before we do that.

Break

Alan Granadino

Welcome back to the seminar. It has so far been very interesting. And now we are going to shift our focus slightly and we are going to deal with North-South collaboration and also focus a little bit more on social democratic movements in northern and southern Europe. Before starting I think we had a question from Monica Quirico.

[connection problem with Monica Quirico]

Alan Granadino

No, we cannot hear you. So maybe we just read the question. Larsson and Mr Lykketoft you both have given a quite radical definition of the Swedish-Danish model. Mr Lykketoft, in Marxian terms, what was left of this pretty socialist inspiration in the 1990s? Mr Larsson, wrote in 1991, "we have learned the lesson. Full employment is no longer our priority."

[laughter]

Allan Larsson

Who said that?

Thorsten Borring Olesen

You did, allegedly you did.

[laughter]

Allan Larsson

No. No, I think this is a complete misunderstanding. Complete misunderstanding. It is a sort of way that very conservative people try to oppose our politics. When I was the Minister for Finance, we had an inflation rate of 10 percent, 8–10 percent. We lost jobs throughout the country everyday. So, inflation was the big threat to employment. Therefore, we had to cope with that. And I formulated the sentence in the finance bill about this saying that "in order to safeguard employment and welfare, we have to fight inflation." That was the sentence. But those who were opposing me, they cut off the first part. "In order to safeguard employment and welfare." They cut it out and said you are only fighting inflation.

We had a very successful operation on inflation. So instead of having draconian economic measures, we appointed a group of former negotiators and mediators. They formed a group and negotiated a national contract for the whole labour market and brought inflation down from ten to three percent. We based that on experience from Finland. Finland had done that. We learned from them. So, within that, that was a way to safeguard jobs, employment and welfare. So now you know it. So never use that phrase again.

[laughter]

Mogens Lykketoft

The question was also, how much we were influenced by Marxist thinking back in the 60s and 70s and so on. I think I can quote one of my good friends, whom I was a colleague with in government, said once "we have a lot, much, to thank Marx for, but there is not much of Marx left in our nowadays thinking." And that goes particularly for the idea of state ownership or for the means of production. But on the other hand you can say that in the late 1960s, beginning of 1970s, both in Denmark and in Sweden, there were a lot of discussion and proposals from the labour movement about profit sharing schemes of a kind, trying also to change the very unequal distribution of wealth and income, particularly in the ownership of the means of production. First to say, we were not very successful with that part of our political initiatives. There is something left in the way we finally reached the design of the labour market pension schemes. But the original ideas did not catch fire and support in the political arena during the 1970s and later on. I regret that, but that is a fact. So, it was a new Keynesian policy of a kind, it was the conviction that we could maintain and improve an equal distribution of living conditions through public intervention in providing services and having high taxation. That is not, I think, very Marxist. But that is what we were able to do, also in a political environment where, at least in Denmark, the Social Democratic Party never had a majority of its own.

Alan Granadino

Thank you very much for your answers. Now we move on. We will start talking a little bit about this North-South collaboration. Joaquín Almunia, you have mentioned before something that has been very interesting for me, which is that you had a high opinion of international solidarity developed by the Nordics. This is one dimension that maybe I can ask you something about more specifically later. But connected to that, the first question that I would like to ask is – in the introduction to the seminar we have mentioned the collaboration established between Spanish and Nordic Social Democrats during and after the transition to democracy in Spain – so I wanted to ask you, if you were somehow involved in this collaboration and if not, if you were aware of it? And after that I would like to ask you what were the main characteristics of this cooperation?

Joaquín Almunia

During the years of Franco's regime, the dictatorship, we the Spaniards in general, the democrats in Spain and in particular the two organizations linked with the Social Democratic Movement – that is, the PSOE as a political party, member of the Socialist International and the *Unión General de Trabajadores*, UGT, as member of the CIOSL,[14] the World Organization of Trade Unions and since 1983 of the European Confederation of Trade Unions – we were in very close contact with parties of the Socialist International or unions of similar orientation and in particular with parties and unions in the Scandinavian countries, as well as Germans, both the SPD and the DGB and other organizations.[15]

But I remember particularly the good cooperation, support, solidarity of those areas, the Scandinavian countries and Germany. What kind of cooperation? In some cases, financial support for illegal parties or for illegal unions. We needed financial support to survive from this point of view, to try to maintain some kind of organizations within Spain and support in terms of training, sharing experiences, opening doors, supporting members of our organizations when they were arrested and so on. It was extremely important for us, this helped us in our difficult activities.

They helped us also to have the doors open to the democratic world. This was very, very important for us to prepare our strategies and our priorities, that the dictatorship would come to an end. So at the beginning of the transition, in the beginning of 1976, when both the Socialist Party, PSOE, and the union UGT were established in a very weak way, but established in some offices and in Madrid, we had a clear view of the priorities of our actions to be prepared for the first elections and the first collective bargaining activities in a free environment. I think it was extremely useful. And it is a pity, that now in these difficult days again for other Europeans, the Socialist International, for instance, is not as strong as it was at the time of Olof Palme,[16] Willy

---

[14] This is the Spanish acronym for The International Confederation of Free Trade Unions (ICFTU)

[15] SPD, the Social Democratic Party of Germany. DGB is the German Trade Union Confederation.

[16] Olof Palme was Prime Minister of Sweden from 1969 to 1976 and from 1982 to 1986.

Brandt,[17] Bruno Kreisky[18] and others. But in particular these three leaders were perfectly well known in Spain.

I very well remember Olof Palme making a campaign against Franco's dictatorship, and when there were executions of some people in the last months of Franco's life, Olof Palme was strongly criticized here by the official press and by the official establishment. But all the Spaniards beyond the limits of our political organizations and the union membership, thanked Olof Palme for this strong, well-organized example of solidarity and support for those who were suffering the consequences of the dictatorship. These are things that we will never forget in our life.

Alan Granadino

Thank you very much. Now the same question for Allan, would you like to reply?

Allan Larsson

I think I can from my point of view confirm what Joaquín said, that we had very strong relations between the Swedish Social Democratic Party and the Spanish Socialists. And Olof Palme was, as you said, a very strong leader in this respect.

I remember also the Portuguese revolution and when the leaders came to Sweden to see how to build democracy. And they asked the trade union leader at that time how long it takes to implement a national law on codetermination? And the President of the Swedish TUC[19] said that, well it can take 10–20 years before we have it fully implemented. And they thought it could be done in two, three weeks. So, there were quite different perspectives between the Iberian and Scandinavian regions.

Nevertheless, we had very good relations and that was continued over the years, when PSOE came to office and Felipe Gon-

---

[17] Willy Brandt was Chancellor of the Federal Republic of Germany from 1969 to 1974.

[18] Bruno Kreisky was Chancellor of Austria from 1970 to 1983.

[19] Sweden's Trades Unions' Congress. In Swedish is the *Landsorganisationen i Sverige* (LO)

zalez came to see Olof Palme and then Ingvar Carlsson[20] later took over these contacts. I remember we had a meeting in Harpsund, the place where the Prime Minister goes on weekends. And so, I had a weekend with Felipe in Stockholm. That was in the beginning of the 1990s and that was before our application for membership in the EU. So, we discussed very much the modalities for Sweden becoming a member, and then we had all the support from Spain, when we finally did that. So there has been a long process of close relationship, where we hopefully have given some inspiration, but we also got support, which we also will remember from that time.

Mogens Lykketoft

Joaquín said a lot of kind words about the Nordic countries and Nordic Social Democratic Parties supporting international solidarity. I think that – of course it has been expressed in a high level of international development assistance support for the United Nations and so on – but I have to say with regret that the attitude in Denmark toward immigration, refugees, has been much more problematic and hostile among the population and also put a mark on our own party and their policies in recent times.

But it is still a fact that the Nordic countries are contributing pretty much more than nearly every other part of the world to international development assistance. The other remark, I should say, about this in the past, is that I agree that it was very important that we had in the 70s and a couple of decades further on, a rather strong Socialist International, represented by people like Willy Brandt in the chair and later on António Guterres.[21] That has more or less disappeared. We have had a strong cooperation within the European Union. I think that my boss in government Poul Nyrup Rasmussen did a lot of good work with the Party of European Socialists being more important as a transnational

---

[20] Ingvar Carlsson was Prime Minister of Sweden from 1986 to 1991 and from 1994 to 1996.

[21] António Guterres was President of the Socialist International from 1999 to 2005, he was also Prime Minister of Portugal from 1995 to 2002, and since 2017 he is the Secretary General of the United Nations.

entity. I think that is what I can say in this connection. One thing more: I have always envied the Swedish Social Democratic Party for their very strong party secretariat on international affairs. You have had much, much more direct contact with Third World countries, liberation movements and so on, than we have been able to maintain. Even if we have a common history, I think, for international solidarity, even back to the 60s by supporting, for instance, the freedom resistance in Southern Africa.

Alan Granadino

Thank you. So, I will stay a little bit with this topic. I will follow up on one of the comments, that Joaquín Almunia said. You highlighted the fact that German Social Democrats and the Nordics also were especially supportive, during the years of the transition to democracy. Even before. And you have mentioned the areas of financial support and also formation and education of militance, which are two relevant areas. I would like to ask you, in your opinion, this kind of support, did it influence the ideological and the strategic line of the party, of the PSOE. Because at that time there were other models available, the French model for example, of the union of the left, union between socialists and communists. And Spain was moving toward democracy with a strong communist party. We were not sure of how strong it would be, but during the dictatorship it had gained a reputation of being the main party in opposition. And something similar was happening in Portugal. So, was this somehow relevant for the ideological line of the party?

Joaquín Almunia

You are right, before we started to vote in a democracy, the first democratic election took place in June 1977. The first time I had voted for almost 30 years! We were not allowed to really vote before. Only in our university struggles, we organized assemblies to vote. So, at that time both for the party, for the PSOE, and for the union, the UGT, the Friedrich Ebert Foundation,[22] linked to the SPD, was extremely useful. I mentioned before the economic support that was needed, but the training carried out by the [Friedrich] Ebert Foundation, also in Lisbon by the way, in Portugal, and in Madrid, in Spain, was extremely useful.

I said at the beginning I started in 1976 as an economist of the Union. The activities organized by the Ebert Foundation here in Madrid or in other parts of Spain, to explain what a union works with in a democratic environment, how to organize industrial relations, how to develop techniques for collective bargaining… any of the activities that were not known by us living under dictatorship, were extremely useful. It was explained by the Ebert Foundation that organized seminars, organized conferences, brought to Spain experts, promoted exchanges of views, etc. We also travelled to Germany and it was extremely useful. And of course, the same in the case of the PSOE at the political level. Extremely useful.

What else did we receive? We received support from others, of course. I mentioned the Scandinavian countries, but I did not mention before the Belgian Socialists, the PvdA in the Netherlands, even the Labour Party, before they started a revolution with Michael Foot[23] toward surrealist policies. We had a lot of contacts, a lot of changes. It was extremely interesting, not only being allowed to go to the congresses and to the meetings to explain what the situation was like, and what were our needs, but to learn. Extrememly useful. And this was not so easy with our neighbours France and Italy. Why? On the one hand, because the French Socialist Party before Mitterrand[24] was very, very weak. As it is the case nowadays again. And the Mitterrand party was in this theory of *union de la gauche*.[25] And we did not share this theory. The

---

[22] It is a German political foundation associated with the German Social Democratic party SPD.

[23] He was the leader of the British Labour Party from 1980 to 1983.

[24] François Mitterrand was President of France from 1981 to 1995.

[25] The union of the left (1972–77). It was an alliance between the French Socialist party, the French Communist Party and the Radical Party of the Left that included a common program.

Communist Party in Spain was supposed to be very strong before the elections. And was weaker and weaker since the moment we started to vote. And we did not want to do this.

We won the first elections in 1982 with a big majority. We did not need to organize coalitions and all this. And in Italy, the case was a strong Italian Communist Party, that was a different animal, a much more pro-European under Berlinguer[26] than the French Communist and all this. But Italian politics was so complex, that it was difficult to find good inspiration in the way that the Italian politics developed. With all my respects and sympathy to Italians, who are fantastic and very close to us from many points of view, but from the political point of view, it was not easy for us to find inspirations in Italian politics.

Alan Granadino

Very interesting. Thank you very much. So now a question for everyone. Could we say that the Spanish and also the Portuguese cases of cooperation were outstanding cases of the Nordic Social Democratic transnational activities in Europe in the 1970s and 80s, or was it just one or two cases among the many transnational activities occurring among European Social Democrats at that time?

Allan Larsson

If I understand the question… If there are other such cooperation? I would say that Greece was such a case for us. When the generals took over Greece in 1967, I think, a lot of the politically active Socialists in Greece, they emigrated to Scandinavia – Sweden, a lot of them – and they formed their own political organizations here – a platform to work to recover or retain, to take back power in Greece. There has been a very strong link between Swedish Social Democrats and Greek Socialists over the years.

---

[26] Enrico Berlinguer was General Secretary of the Italian Communist Party from 1972 to 1984.

Mogens Lykketoft

I think that the experiences are more or less the same. For instance, I was Foreign Minister at the same time as the young Yorgos Papandreou[27] was Foreign Minister in Greece. He was really a half-Swede, actually, because he lived part of his youth in Sweden, in migration, and as the Swedes did, we tried to make connections with the new party of the Papadreou family in the 1960s and 1970s. But I think Spain, Portugal and Greece were one and the same thing in our understanding of the necessities to support democratic and socialist development in those new members of the European community. And that was a much more vivid exercise than later on, when we expanded the European Union to the East, because the specific Social Democratic Parties always were very weak and distant from us compared with the cooperation we had established with Greece, Portugal and Spain during the 60s and 70s.

Thorsten Borring Olesen

Just a very short and very technical question. When you study the Socialist International in its early days, it was obvious that a lot of negotiations and debates and so on, contexts, were actually negotiated in German. But later on, I mean when you met in the 1980s, what was the language? Because I guess that English was not in vivid circulation as it is today. So how did you manage to communicate?

Joaquín Almunia

In our case with a bad management of languages. We tried to use English or French. It depends on what kind of second language we had at school. But you are right: French was still present in international discussions. I think the translation in the official meetings were both to French and to English, from different languages. Probably German, which while the logical language at the

---

[27] Yorgos Papandreou was the Greek Minister of Foreign Affairs from 1999 to 2004 and from 2009 to 2010. He was also Prime Minister of Greece from 2009 to 2011.

beginning of the history of Socialist International, was lost by the time of the 70s. I really do not remember if… Personally, I communicated more in French, that in fact is my second language, or in English, which at that time was even worse than the second one.

Thorsten Borring Olesen
But the problem, of course, was that the Nordics, we are not very good at French.

Joaquín Almunia
But you are very good in all languages.

Allan Larsson
It was easy to talk to you Joaquín because you could speak English. But when I met Felipe, he was speaking French and then we had translation.

Joaquín Almunia
Felipe has not tried to learn English, and even now he has still not, now that he is 80 years old. He has a fantastic capacity to get information that is only available in English and he is informed. I do not know why. What are the techniques that he uses?

Allan Larsson
Google Translate.

Joaquín Almunia
Probably.

Alan Granadino
We have another question from one of the co-organizers of the seminar. Andreas, if you want, please.

Andreas Mørkved Hellenes
I'll just add that a number of the prominent players of the Swedish Social Democratic Party, at least in international affairs, they were

francophone in the 1970s and 1980s, including Olof Palme, whose French was not bad at all. My question also has a bit to do with France, and more specifically with the significance of Jacques Delors,[28] and I wanted to know if anyone can say anything about Delors' significance for how Scandinavian social democracy saw Brussels before and during the Swedish membership negotiations? Because as an expert and politician in France, Delors was known as someone who had openly expressed his affinities with Scandinavian social democracy, which made him sort of an odd man out in French socialism. So, were there informal contacts with Delors or through the Socialist International networks to facilitate an understanding between the Scandinavians – and here I include the Norwegians as well, because it was the ambition of Brundtland's government to take Norway into the EU – so between these Scandinavian governments, social democratic governments, and Brussels?

Allan Larsson

Can I start answering that question? I hope that Mogens can say more. But from my point of view, the Swedish point of view, Jacques Delors had an enormous role in presenting the European Union, or the EEC as it was called at that time, with a new dimension. That was the social dimension. It was not only the market. It was the social dimension. There is no Europe without the social dimension, was his message. That was in the 1980s, when we started to realize that this European Union was something other than what we had seen until then. So, without that, we had not had difficulties to convince our party comrades. And he was the one, who opened the door for the EU-negotiations in 1989. And then he also accepted, he was somewhat hesitant to open for membership-negotiations. So, the Austrian application, I think it was early in 1990, was put on ice. And it was when Sweden in the autumn, the same year, applied, that he opened for negotiations with the EFTA countries. But he had an enormous role. And he used to

---

[28] Jacques Delors was President of the European Commission from 1985 to 1995.

present himself as a Social Democrat, not as a French Socialist. In this way, it was easy to discuss with him.

Mogens Lykketoft

I think I have very much the same impression of the importance of Jacques Delors, as having close relations with our leading foreign policy actors, European policy actors in the 1980s and 1990s. I was not so much personally involved in that. I was in economics at the time. But Jacques Delors helped, as Allan just said, the understanding of the European project in the rank and file of the Social Democrats in Denmark, exactly by saying, telling or showing that it was not only about economics, it was also about social and environmental cooperation that could raise common standards. That was very important. There was another Social Democrat I came to know even better: Michel Rocard,[29] who was also a Social Democrat in France. And for a short time also Prime Minister as we remember. But maybe he was not either totally in line with the mainstream of the French Socialist Party. Nowadays I really do not know what the mainstream of the French Socialist Party is.

Joaquín Almunia

I can say a lot about Jacques Delors. He is a very, very good friend of Spain and the Spanish PSOE during these years. He knows perfectly well what is going on here. Jacques Delors, it's true, that was not the typical French Socialist. He came from a different origin than the core of the SFIO Party, and Mitterrand's ideas. He came from the Christian side, from the Christian unionism of CFDT; he came from the centre-left, not from the traditional socialism in the party. He was always, and he is still, every time that he speaks from time to time in public – he is 95 years old – he is always in favour of this social dimension of the European integration, of the European project, and of social dialogue. He pays a lot of attention to what is going on at the level of the social partners. He has always been like this. And it is a pity that this

---

[29] Michel Rocard was Prime Minister of France from 1988 to 1991.

vision of how Europe should combine political ambitions, social dimensions and economic efficiency, is not more present in many of the present leaders, even of the present leaders of the European Socialist Party – which I think is not doing a very good job, at the present time. Unfortunately, it was not the case in Delors' years, durig the 1980s and the 1990s, but now the Conservatives, the Centre-Right Party, the Popular Party in Europe,[30] has much more coordination and substance as a political party than the Party of the European Socialists. Unfortunately.

Alan Granadino

Thank you very much. Time is going very quickly, and we have now in seven minutes another break. And then we are going to move on and discuss more about the European integration topics.

But before that, I would like to just pick up one of the things that Mary commented upon, at the beginning of this seminar, and that also Joaquín talked about. I would like to ask you about if the Nordic model was used, this concept, for referring to different policy areas, for example foreign policy.

Joaquín mentioned the solidarity dimension of the Nordic foreign policy. There is a strong link between that foreign policy and a social democratic system. But it also has a link to the policies of neutrality. And in this sense, I would like to ask you if for Spain and for Spanish Socialists, which in the 1980s were still considering that the best option for Spain perhaps would be to remain neutral internationally and not to join NATO. If the Nordic countries and specifically the Nordic balance, the idea of the Nordic balance, was relevant or influential for thinking about the position or the role of Spain in world affairs after the transition to democracy? I have read that Emilio Menéndez del Valle[31] developed the idea of the Iberian balance mirroring the Nordic balance. So, could you tell us something about that?

---

[30] Almunia is here referring to the European People's Party.

[31] Emilio Menéndez del Valle was PSOE's expert in international policy in the 1970s.

Joaquín Almunia

I know very well Emilio, but I did not read what he wrote on this. But as for my view on this: well, for historical reasons Spain was not involved in any of the two World Wars during the past century. And at the end of the second World War, in the aftermath of the war, Spain was under Franco's dictatorship, so did not participate in the organization of the international community after the war.

But in 1953, Franco's regime passed agreements with the US, with Eisenhower,[32] who was the President of the US, and one of the elements of these agreements was the establishment in Spanish territory of three military bases for the Americans. So, we did not want this kind of submission of national interest of Spain under the leadership of the US in the times of the Cold War. As democrats, we were politically against the communist system, clearly. So, we were not tempted to establish a balance between Washington and Moscow, at any time. We were pro-West of course, politically. But we were not pro-American, pro-North American. We considered that North America should eliminate this presence in our territory.

The centrist government in 1981 decided unilaterally against our political will in parliament to join NATO. We were against joining NATO with a presence of American bases, American military bases, in our territory and without revising the conditions under which in those bases nuclear arms were to be kept. So, we were against this accession to NATO. The way the centrist government did in 1981.

So, we promised in our electoral platform for the elections in 1982, to organize a referendum about the presence in NATO. Once we were in government, we kept the compromise to organize a referendum, but in this referendum our position was yes, let us remain in NATO, but under different conditions. Three of four different conditions, that were supported by the parliament. So, we were happy belonging to NATO, given that the conditions were fulfilled. And now this is no more a discussion in the main-

---

[32] Dwight D. Eisenhower was President of the United States of America from 1953 to 1960.

stream parties in Spain. Only the radicals from the left and from the right put into question NATO membership.

And now during these terrible days of the Ukrainian War, even those opinions are becoming more and more minoritarian. So, I think this debate came to an end, but we never organized our thinking on NATO, based on this third way approach of some countries, such as Sweden or Finland or Austria, that were neutral countries. We never considered Spain as a neutral country.

Alan Granadino

Thank you very much. Now would be the time for a short break.

Break

Thorsten Borring Olesen

We will take now this third turn in our conversation and we will now turn to what we could call the Nordic model in Europe and Europe in the Nordic model. So, I will actually start by presenting myself, because I do not think I did that in the beginning. My name is Thorsten Borring Olesen, I am Professor of Contemporary History here at the University of Aarhus.

But I return to Delors and take our point of departure there, because as you know in the 1980s it was very common to depict the European project and the EC as a neoliberal project. Then in the 1990s it was turned a social democratic project. And Delors served as a bridge, you could say, between the two. But in Denmark at least, Delors in the 1980s was not a very popular man, because, in social democrat circles and to the left, Delors was considered to be the one who actually progressed the single European market without a social dimension. And later on, he very much focused on the social dimension. In the beginning of the 1990s, he was the one that put up a strong argument for actually putting in a social dimension into European integration and into the new EU coming in. What is your reflection on that and on Delors' role in that?

Joaquín Almunia

Let me start, if you wish. As I said before, Delors has always, when he was a French politician, Minister for Finance, and before he became a Minister with Mitterrand, he was always in favor of social dialogue and of the social dimension of economic policies. This is the Delors I knew, the Delors books I read: he has always been like this. The question is that in the 1980s in his first years as the President of the Commission, the main priority was to achieve the single market. By definition, the achievement of the single market is a project based on elimination of barriers and promoting the free movement of citizens, but also free movement of goods, services and capital.

These were the days, when not only the single market was starting to be built, there was a project that received the support not only from Delors, but also from Margaret Thatcher, for instance. But they were the years of the liberalization of the movement of capital. They were the years when the Asian tigers, the Koreans, and Singapore, and others emerged. They were years where still the Reagan and Thatcher ideological platforms were predominant. And at the end of this decade, Delors turned the massive treaty negotiations and the launch of the Economic and Monetary Union, the building of the Euro area.

So, it is true, that there were moments of predominance of neoliberal thoughts, but he has always been a voice drawing the attention of the political leaders in Europe about the need to complement this view with social dialogue with the social dimension of Europe. Always. And even before the thoughts on the social dimension, he was against an Economic and Monetary Union where the monetary pillar was predominant above the economic pillar. And he considered that economic policy coordination was absolutely needed to strengthen the social cohesion within the EU and so on. I do not share this view of Delors as being a monetarist or neocon… No, absolutely not. Never. And why did he not succeed in the building of a real social dimension of Europe? Because of the political leaders of Europe sitting at the European Council. They were not in favor of this. And I have to say that some of the Scandinavian leaders sitting around the table of the European Council after the accession of Sweden and Finland, were not supporting these social dimension initiatives. Because, in my personal view, I have the feeling that some of Scandinavian leaders feared that the social Europe will diminish the strength of the Scandinavian welfare states. Having to equalize, to find the average of social protection of social rights, of social policies, between the more advanced in Europe – that were the Scandinavians – and the less advanced, that at that time were the Southern Europeans.

I have this feeling, but it was not the only obstacle to advance toward the social dimension of Europe. Allan Larsson has worked on this, not only as Director-General but after, when he received the mandate to think about this social dimension. And for sure, he will have a clear view on this.

Allan Larsson

Yes, perhaps I share your views of the first part on Delors, that he had a full agenda on the single act – Single European Act – and of the EMU. And, therefore, his social agenda came a bit later. And it came mainly through the White Paper, developed in 1992–93. That was about the economic policy, but it was also to show the social dimension.

I came in as Director-General in 1995 and stayed there for five years. I can say that Delors' White Paper set the agenda for the work we did. And we made a lot of progress. So, you should not see Delors' role as ending in 1995: he has a long impact on European policies. And particularly on this – which was where I have different opinions than Joaquín – that what Sweden, Finland and Denmark did at that time was to focus on employment, since employment is the basics for the social agenda. And as, at that time, the treaty did not include employment as a matter of common concern, it was not a policy area for the EU. That was in 1997, in Amsterdam, it was the first time that employment was introduced in the treaty as a matter of common concern. And on that we built the two... The Commission was asked then to develop the European employment strategy, and we did it the same year. And it was accepted in the Luxembourg summit. So that is in my view a very strong social dimension that came in through the employment provisions in the treaty. And that was thanks to Delors.

Thorsten Borring Olesen

Yes. Mogens, will you supplement?

Mogens Lykketoft

Yes, not that I can supplement very much. I think my two friends have summed up pretty well what Delors was, what he did. And some reasons why it was not that successful. I think the main responsibility rests, as was said also, with the European Council, the heads of states and government. At the time when social democrats were very much in power: they came into power in Britain; in government in France; Schröder won the German elections;[33] we had a number of Social Democratic governments in the Nordic area… and also otherwise in Europe. My personal view is that the Social Democratic Movement missed an opportunity, at the very top of our influence in all the major councils in Europe: we did not invest that much in developing the social dimension of the European cooperation. We were not that aware either of the climate dimension, which is now so dominant. We have not done enough work to fight tax evasion, which is one of the basic weaknesses of European societies and the welfare state financing. It has been for me in the past 20 years a reason for regret, that when we were so strong, we could not agree on doing much more.

Joaquín Almunia

I fully agree with this missed opportunity of Social Democratic governments in the EU, who were at that time 15 members. We did not have the enlargement coming up soon. So, we were obliged at that time, as Europeans, to think how to deepen the European integration project, supporting better economic policy coor-

---

[33] Gerhard Schröder was Chancellor of Germany from 1998 to 2005.

dination to support the Euro, and to deepen the social dimension of the European integration. But unfortunately, and at that time among the 15 members only Spain and Ireland had Social Democrats or Labour Parties in opposition, 13 out of 15 European countries had Social Democrat Prime Ministers or strong coalitions with relevant presence of Social Democrats – I remember attending meetings as a leader of the opposition in Spain, I was isolated among members in government around the table, together with my Irish good friend – at that time predominated a theory of soft coordination of economic policies and social policies. Soft coordination defined by the Lisbon strategy for growth.

The Lisbon strategy for growth was a very good idea to complement the decision to build an Economic and Monetary Union, but this soft coordination was completely irrelevant. Completely irrelevant, unfortunately. And we were not able to define a real, credible and viable growth strategy for our economies, in a period where many of the economies of the EU were trying to converge toward the fulfilment of the Maastricht criteria. And in some countries, of course in Spain, but in many others, this convergence toward the Maastricht criteria forced some kind of prudent and even restricted macroeconomic policies, to go below the thresholds of inflation and interest rates, deficit, and so on.

It was a real missed opportunity. And only in the aftermath of the financial crisis, a longer mechanism for economic policy coordination has started to exist. The European semester, and now with the next generation of EU funds, the national reformed programs with the list of structural reforms and the list of investment projects that can be funded by European funds. At the same time those funds funded with common issued EU debt. This is a new framework, that should allow us to revise the mistakes that we did 20 years ago.

But unfortunately, those mistakes are now in an environment of weaker Social Democratic Parties, complex coalitions in most of our countries, difficulties in having clear platforms to advance coordinated actions, and now of course the consequences of the pandemic and the consequences of the Ukrainian War, which are creating additional difficulties for our economy. So, I fully agree with this. I think it is a point that should be underlined from the social democratic point of view.

Mary Hilson

I just wanted to follow up. Joaquín Almunia, you have said why you think this opportunity was missed, and it was partly due to convergence in the Maastricht criteria. And you also said something about the Social Democratic leaders, the Nordic countries' leaders after accession. But I actually wanted to ask Mogens and Allan your views about why?

Allan Larsson

I think that you should not see the Lisbon strategy as negative as you described it, Joaquín. I think it is more that the implementation of it failed. And it failed partly because we were in the, let's say, high days of the neoliberal wave, that imploded in 2008. But these years, from 2000 to 2008, they were some sort of heyday for the neoliberal agenda, and it was not easy in individual countries to run a strong social agenda. But the policy, the priorities, they were well designed in the Lisbon agenda, but not fulfilled, not translated. And then you remember who came after as the President of the Commission, and he had a very right-wing agenda for the EU.

Joaquín Almunia

Yes of course Allan, but my criticism is not toward the wording and the priorities written down in the original document of the Lisbon strategy. I fully agree with this strategy on paper. The problem is that the governments around the table of the European Council were not ready to coordinate themselves in a serious way to implement the priorities and the strategies embedded in the Lisbon strategy. I know that Barroso as the President of the Commission was Right-wing, but the failure of this strategy had started before Barroso came. I had spent the last year of the Prodi Commission[34] as a member of the college, because Solbes[35] had been appointed Vice President in Spain, and I substituted Pedro Solbes, and during the last year of the Prodi Commission, with fantastic members around the table of this college, there was a common feeling of the failure of the Lisbon strategy. Before Barroso could even consider becoming one day a member of the European Commission.

Mogens Lykketoft

I do not think, frankly, that it was in the late 1990s so much the Scandinavian Social Democrats being afraid of diminishing their own social model that we did not embark on a more progressive effort toward the European social dimension. I think on the other hand, that we have not mentioned how the German attitude toward economic policy did not change that much from the Kohl[36] government to the Schröder government; and later on actually also, when you had the Social Democrats in German government coalitions up to the Covid crisis, Germany was a stopping factor in almost any kind of European solidarity.

We saw that during the financial crisis, after that the treatment of Greece, and so on. Our opinion about European solidarity did not have much support from differently colored German governments over time, until finally Merkel[37] gave in, in the great package during the Covid crisis.

So, that is maybe more important than anything else. The other factor is that even during the Labour government in Britain, Britain was not that engaged in European integration, not even on the social front, as far as I have been able to follow. And with these two major players not interested in greater European solidarity, it would have been difficult anyway.

---

[34] Here Almunia refers to the European Commission presided by Romano Prodi from 1999 to 2004.

[35] Pedro Solbes is a Spanish economist that has been European Commissioner for Economic and Monetary Affairs (1999–2004), Minister of Economy and Finance of Spain (2004–2009) and Vice President of Spain (also 2004–2009).

[36] Helmut Kohl was Chancellor of Germany from 1982 to 1998.

[37] Angela Merkel was Chancellor of Germany from 2005 to 2021.

Thorsten Borring Olesen

I would like to continue a bit here, because I think Joaquín had a good point in the sense that why did we not exploit the kind of majority that we had in the 1990s. And why were the Nordic Social Democrats maybe not more active?

You mentioned yourself also the tax evasion aspect of it. But in my interpretation, I think also the Nordic Social Democrats to a certain degree were hampered by the fact that they knew that the Nordic populations were not that supranational-orientated in European affairs. And therefore, that each time they had to pursue policies in the EU, they had to do it on this intergovernmental level and not taking the bold steps, because they were afraid that they could not carry the day at home.

And I think there is a very interesting aspect related to when the Danes voted no to Maastricht in 1992. I actually think that in the first instance this helped to put the employment agenda right up, because just after the Danish no and the small French yes – at the first summit in Birmingham after that in 1992 – Jacques Delors presented a full analysis of the legitimacy problems of the EU. And one of them was from then on to focus on employment, which became the White Paper, which were put upfront in 1993.

But on the other hand, I think there is also a legacy from losing that kind of referendum, and Denmark lost one more in 2000, and Sweden lost one in 2003 related to the EMU. So, I think there is a double bind here, which on the one hand could promote a Nordic agenda in the EU, but on the other hand also restricted the Nordic governments, especially of the Social Democrat brand, of actually going as far as they wanted to. How do you see that?

Mogens Lykketoft

I just now came to remember that there was, during my short period as party leader, there was a European meeting among party leaders, where I said as follows: "From the Danish experience, if you do not have an explicit, constitutional requirement for having referendums on European issues, never, never, never do it."

[laughter]

Mogens Lykketoft

Because it will always be on very complicated issues, where people vote for very different reasons. How do you like the present government? And will it impact my old age pension? Things like that which have actually nothing to do with it. So that may not sound that democratic, but it is still my opinion that we should try to avoid referenda if we want to expand the European cooperation. But there is another dimension here, Torsten, and that is if we are successful in creating European action on the most progressive issues – like tax evasion, like climate nowadays – we may be able to popularize the idea of closer European cooperation. And some of the fatigue also expressed in Danish referenda over time has been why are we going to support this, when other things that we think is more important that Europe is taking care of is not on the agenda, or not lifted politically?

Joaquín Almunia

May I put a question to my Scandinavian colleagues? I was wondering to what extent the constitution of the Euro-area with at the beginning twelve member states, nowadays 19 member states, but without the presence of Sweden and Denmark – for different reasons I will not discuss the reasons – but to what extent this absence of Sweden and Denmark outside the Eurogroup and the core of the European integration around the Euro area has diminished the possibilities to positively influence the decisions of the EU at large on the social dimension and on the development of the most positive aspects of the welfare states in the Scandinavian countries and the Nordic model?

To what extent this absence of the core, in the core of Europe, is a problem, not only for the countries that want to be there and are not there, but for all of us? For instance, to what extent the austerity orientation led by Germany, Merkel and Wolfgang Schäuble,[38] of course, at the beginning of the debt crisis in 2010,

---

[38] Wolfgang Schäuble was German Minister of Finance from 2009 to 2017.

would have been possible with a stronger presence of the Scandinavian governments and Ministers for Finance in the Eurogroup or in the Euro area decisions?

Mogens Lykketoft

I think you are perfectly right. That is a pity for exactly those reasons, that we are not there. It is not a very big problem for our economy, because we are for all practical reasons apart from the Euro system, just paying for exchange of money and we have no influence. And that is the most important part of the problem, I would say, that we are acting exactly as if we were members of the Eurogroup, but we are not exercising any kind of influence on the Euro economic policy.

Allan Larsson

I doubt that Sweden and Denmark would have changed the course of Europe. I think it was a strong international trend in that. Now, Sweden agreed on the EMU in the negotiations with one condition. That it is up to the parliament to make the decision. And then it was brought to the parliament in the form of a referendum. So, Sweden called the referendum. The Prime Minister Göran Persson[39] was strongly in favour of EMU, but the majority said no. And, therefore, there has been no way in which Sweden could become a member of the third step of EMU. That is a matter of fact. Then does that mean, that we are not on board on policy making? Not at all. Not at all. When the big package was put together in the Covid crisis, Sweden was very welcome to pay much more than we would get back. So, we are a perfect member for the others, that we are net contributor and we are welcomed to the table at these times.

Joaquín Almunia

I was not referring, Allan, to the decisions as a consequence of the pandemic. I was thinking more in 2010, where the public debt crisis exploded in Greece and spilled over to other Euro area eco-

---

[39] Göran Persson was Prime Minister of Sweden from 1996 to 2006.

nomies, triggering harsh austerity mandates under the leadership of Germany and followed unfortunately by France in the Euro-group. Nobody else was there with clear arguments against this harsh austerity, unless the country was suffering the consequences of the public debt crisis. And this created, in my view – and I was there as a member of the Commission, but no more as the Commissioner for Economic Affairs – this created a big distortion with strong social consequences for the Greek people in particular, and the strong political consequences for the support of the European project around the territory of the EU. And I hoped that if Sweden and Denmark would have been there, I'm sure you would have been able to moderate the…

Allan Larsson
Sorry, the problem is that between 2006 and 2014 we had a right-wing government that was an extremely market oriented government. It would not have helped at all if we had been a member of the EMU core group at that time.

Joaquín Almunia
Yes. But when I listen to guys like Carl Bildt[40] or the guy who was a Finance Minister at that time,[41] I cannot remember the name, or others, or some Finnish politicians from the centre-right, I consider them more centre-oriented, than when I listen to their colleagues in the Popular Party in Southern European countries or in other countries. So, I would have more confidence on even the centre-right politicians in Sweden than in another countries.

Thorsten Borring Olesen
But there is a very interesting historical development here, because as a historian, and if you go back to the 1950s, in the OEEC, you would see the Danish government stand up there and

---

[40] Carl Bildt was Prime Minister of Sweden from 1991 to 1994 and Minister for Foreign Affairs from 2006 to 2014. He was member of the Moderate Party.
[41] Almunia is probably referring to Anders Borg, Swedish Minister for Finance from 2006 to 2014. He was member of the Moderate Party.

ask the Germans – who already had built up a strong economy with strong export surpluses – there, and arguing for the Germans to actually import more, because, as it was expressively said, you cannot live from gold. In the 1970s Anker Jørgensen,[42] a new Social Democrat Prime Minister, was saying precisely the same to Helmut Schmidt.[43] 30 years on, no Danish Prime Minister, whether he is a liberal or he is a social democrat, would say that. Why? Because now the Nordic countries perform like Germany. They pursue the same, to a large degree, economic and monetary policy. Is that something that has changed the Nordic model?

Mogens Lykketoft

A difficult question. Yes, you can say it was not that encouraging, even when we had the Covid package accepted, that the Nordic countries – Denmark, Sweden and Finland – were on the restrictive side of the negotiations. That did not change that much, fortunately, but from my point of view it was a wrong position. It can be explained the way you do it – that we have increasingly conformed with Germany over time – but I think it is still a point for discussion, and I am not quite sure we will see a repetition of the Nordic governments being on the restrictive side next time we have to negotiate how to manage economic problems in Europe.

I do not hope so, but I am also a little optimistic that things, during the present crisis of the Russian agression in Ukraine, are gradually changing toward a much better understanding of the need for more European solidarity, not only in defense and security, but in general – in order to be sure that our societies in Europe are resistant against a populist takeover. I mean, we are not free of that danger yet. The French result was good, yes, but more than 40 percent voting for that lady[44] is still frightening. And similar things could happen in other European countries if we do

---

[42] Anker Jørgensen was Prime Minister of Denmark from October 1972 to December 1973.

[43] Helmut Schmidt was Chancellor of the Federal Republic of Germany from 1974 to 1982.

[44] Here Lykketoft is referring to Marine Le Pen, the leader of the French extreme Right party National Rally.

not practice more solidarity in overcoming social problems and unemployment.

Allan Larsson

I am not quite…, where do I start, could you make the question a bit more precise?

Thorsten Borring Olesen

I mean, that the crux of the question of course is that is it like this, that the way the Nordic countries pursue economic policy these days has changed from the good Keynesian times into having this fixed exchange rate – which Denmark is stronger on than Sweden, I know, but still a lot of the basic ingredients in the foreign economic policies that have been pursued by Denmark and Sweden are to a large degree the same? And, also, I think it is very linked to the German success formula.

Allan Larsson

I think that the views on economic policies are very much influenced by the more general, what I call, the long waves. It was an end, an abrupt end in 2008. And then the international organizations like IMF and OECD and others have started to rethink and they have also criticized the history of their policies. So, there is a new room for it – it does not come from individual countries, it comes from this set of international organizations that create the framework for our policies. And that is a new theme, and I think that is what Social Democrats and the left in general should take on board, and try to strengthen, because the message is quite different nowadays than it was 10 years ago.

That is my reading of it: rather go that way, than pointing out individual countries. I think that our discussion in Sweden is, should we have a more expansive economic policy? The problem is that we have a high rate of employment and we have difficulties to fill vacancies. So, if we have expanded general demand more, then we would have even more difficulties to fill the vacancies. So is the question of how we can better integrate those people who are coming to us as refugees and bring them into employment. But that is another sort of policies, that is a very specific role for active labour market and social policies, rather than general demand policies.

Thorsten Borring Olesen

But it feeds back to, I mean, the whole issue of what we are debating here about the Nordic model. As you are probably well aware, 10 years ago *The Economist* featured a cover on the Nordic model and argued that to a large degree there was a new Nordic model. So, my question here would be, how do you see EU membership for the Nordic countries? I think I can include Norway as well, because Norway is also in the single market. Has the Nordic model changed due to membership, or is it like this, that we can say that some of the basic tenets of the Nordic model have influenced the EU?

Mogens Lykketoft

I think it is both, it is a combination. But that brings me to a remark also about Germany. When we see Germany changing, it would be more likely that also the Nordic countries would change from the very restrictive attitude to European solidarity, so to say. And I think that all the most recent events – Covid, the war – have brought Germany to rethink, and also brought the Nordic countries a step back towards our traditional model, also seen on the European level. But I agree with Allan: it is very much supported by new voices from the World Bank, from the IMF, from the OECD, that the whole framework of economic thinking is changing. I think the recent international events will support that also.

Allan Larsson

If you look at a Swedish opinion, I would say that about 2/3 of the Swedish population would say that Sweden benefits from being a member of the European Union. And that is one of the highest figures in Europe. When we entered, we had 52 percent versus 48, like France on the EMU. So, we can see that there is a support for

Europe as it is today, and it has gone through the Covid period and now we are supporting Ukraine through EU, and so on.

So, there is a strong Swedish support for Europe, as it has developed. And when I tell my Swedish friends that when we had a referendum back in 1994 on what Europe was at that time and we see what Europe is today, it is a dramatically more developed Europe than we have today. And we have still a much higher support for this new Europe. So that is one way of describing it.

Then to say, how much has it influenced Sweden? Yes, a lot of course. For example, we have European trade policy and many other fields, and that has been in many ways positive. Take for example the research and innovation framework programs, which we have benefitted from. Take for example the new research infrastructures that we are building, Sweden and Denmark together. So, we have had a lot of advantages from this.

So therefore, of course, we have been shaped by being a member. But we have also contributed, without selling the whole model, but we have done it in different parts of policy development.

Mary Hilson
Can we take any questions from anybody else?

Joaquín Almunia
I can put a question, that does not need to be answered today, for historians analyzing the Nordic model and the role of the Social Democrats in building or strengthening this Nordic model. But it applies also to those who are like Spain, outside the Nordic model, but admiring this way. To what extent the lower representation of Social Democrats in the governments and parliaments of the EU – our electoral results were much higher 20 or 25 or 30 years ago than now, as a trend, with the exception of Portugal by the way – to what extent this weakness, this relative weakness of Social Democrats across the world, being members of coalition governments, but sometimes complex coalitions with difficult trade offs and compromises, to what extent this, over the medium to long term, puts at risk the Nordic model?

Mogens Lykketoft

I should try to give a part of an answer to this. First of all, I think, recent developments in the Nordic region and Germany and so on, and Portugal of course in particular, shows us that social democracy has not come to end. The reality of modern European politics is that there is no limit for how far a party can go down and up anymore, because the core electorate is not nearly as strong as it was just some decades ago. So, there is a good chance we see new revivals elsewhere in Europe.

And the other part of my reply to that question is that, if you look at the Danish situation, well Social Democrats are the sole government party, but we are down to a little more than a quarter of the electorate. In the last election, but also at recent opinion polls. But the true parties on the left of us, so to say, are no longer extremists: one of them, you can hardly see the difference between the Social Democrats and the Green Socialists.[45] And even what was the far left, the alliance of all the extremist groups, including the old Communists, is now a rather moderate cooperative party for the Social Democratic government. So, it is not that the amount of the electorate supporting more or less our ideas has decreased very much. And it is interesting that in Denmark at least, but I think that in many other European countries as well, the real extremists are no longer on the left, but on the right.

Peter Stadius

I will comment briefly on this question of the Social Democratic Parties and the future. In Finland we have a fairly strong Green Party that has been in many coalition governments and is now in the government as well. And we have these pretty broad coalitions. But in general terms the decrease of the Social Democratic vote and the increase of the Green Party vote has been usually that educated daughters of both right-wing and Social Democratic voters start voting Green. But now we have a government with many young female party leaders from all the specters and with a Social Democratic Prime Minister, a young woman with a two-

---

[45] The Green Left, in Danish this party is called *Socialistisk Folkeparti.*

year old son, I think. And that might be a little, from this perspective that the question was posed, I think there might be a return of the young, educated female voters in Finland.

[laughter]

Mary Hilson

I think we have had a really fascinating conversation. Three hours have passed very quickly. But I am also aware, that we have been online now for three hours and that is quite a long time, I think. Thank you for joining us, and for a really fascinating and wide-ranging conversation.

References

Byrkjeflot, H. et al. (eds), *The Making and Circulation of Nordic Models, Ideas and Images* (London and New York: Routledge, 2021).

Christiansen, N. F. et al, *The Nordic Model of Welfare. A Historical Reappraisal* (Copenhagen: Museum Tusculanum Press, 2006).

Esping-Andersen, Gøsta, *The Three Worlds of Welfare Capitalism* (Cambridge: Polity, 1990).

Fulla, M., "Put (Southern) Europe to Work. The Nordic Turn of European Socialists in the early 1990s," in A. Granadino, S. Nygård & P. Stadius (eds), *Rethinking European Social Democracy and Socialism. The History of the Centre-Left in Northern and Southern Europe in the Late 20th Century* (London and New York: Routledge, 2022), pp. 48–66.

Granadino, A. & P. Stadius, "Adapting the Swedish Model. PSOE-SAP relations during the Spanish transition to democracy," in H. Byrkjeflot et al. (eds), *The Making and Circulation of Nordic Models, Ideas and Images* (London and New York: Routledge, 2021), pp. 102–123.

Hellenes, A. M., H. A. Ikonomou, C. Marklund & Ada Nissen (eds), "Nordic Nineties," special issue of *Culture Unbound*, Vol. 13, No. 1 (2021).

Kenton, Will, "Nordic Model: Comparing the Economic System to the U.S," Investopedia. https://www.investopedia.com/terms/n/nordic-model.asp.

Madsen, P. K., "'How can it possibly fly?' The Paradox of a Dynamic Labour Market in a Scandinavian Welfare State," in J. L. Campbell, J. A. Hall & O. K. Pedersen (eds), *National Identity and the Varities of Capitalism: The Danish Experience* (Montreal: McGill-Queen's University Press 2006), pp. 321–355.

Marklund, C. & K. Petersen, "Return to Sender: American Images of the Nordic Welfare States and Nordic Welfare State Branding," *European Journal of Scandinavian Studies*, Vol. 43, No. 2 (2013), pp. 245–257.

C. Marklund & J. Olsson, "The Portugal campaign: Swedish cooperative assistance in Portugal after the Carnation Revolution." Paper presented at "Nordic models in global entanglements: Towards a contemporary global history of the Nordic region." Workshop at Comwell Kolding 11–12 November 2021.

Moreno, L., "The Nordic Path of Spain's Mediterranean Welfare," Center for European Studies Working Paper Series, No. 163 (2008).

Musiał, K., *The Roots of the Scandinavian Model. Images of progress in the Era of Modernisation* (Baden-Baden: Nomos, 2002).

Nordics.info, "The Nordic Model." https://nordics.info/themes/the-nordic-model.

Rom Jensen, B., A. M. Hellenes, M. Hilson & C. Marklund, "Modelizing the Nordics: Transdiscursive migrations of Nordic models, c. 1965–2020," *Scandinavian Journal of History* (2022).

Schmidt, W. E., "In a Post-Cold War Era, Scandinavia Rethinks itself," *The New York Times*, February 23 1992. https://www.nytimes.com/1992/02/23/weekinreview/in-a-post-cold-war-era-scandinavia-rethinks-itself.html.

Servan-Schreiber, Jean-Jacques, *Le défi américain* (Paris: Denoël, 1967).

Sørensen, Ø. & B. Stråth (eds), *The Cultural Construction of Norden* (Oslo: Scandinavian University Press, 1997).

Viebrock, E. & J. Clasen, "Flexicurity and welfare reform: A review," *Socio-economic review*, Vol. 7, No. 2 (2009), pp. 305–331.

Wikipedia, "Nordic model." https://en.wikipedia.org/wiki/Nordic_model.

Samtidshistoriska frågor

This series is published by The Institute of Contemporary History (Samtidshistoriska institutet). The series summarizes and discusses important historical events and contemporary issues. Edited transcripts from witness seminars, new research from the university's academic staff as well as conference reports are published as part of the series. Information about the series: https://bibl-app.sh.se/publicationseries/list?id=12

Most of the titles in the series can be downloaded in full text, free of charge, from the Digital Science Archive, DiVA, http://www.diva-portal.se.

Some of the titles in the series have been published in collaboration with CBEES (Center for Baltic and Eastern European Studies) at Södertörn University. Responsible for the work with the publication series is Associate Professor Carl Marklund, carl.marklund@sh.se.

Publication series

1. *Olof Palme i sin tid.* Ed. Kjell Östberg (2001).

2. *Kvinnorörelsen och '68.* Ed. Elisabeth Elgán (2001).

3. *Riv alla murar! Vittnesseminarier om sexliberalismen och om Pockettidningen R.* Ed. Lena Lennerhed (2002).

4. *Löntagarfonderna – en missad möjlighet?* Ed. Lars Ekdahl (2002).

5. *Dagens Nyheter: Minnesseminarium över Sven-Erik Larsson. Vittnesseminarium om DN och '68.* Ed. Alf W. Johansson (2003).

6. *Kvinnorna skall göra det! Den kvinnliga medborgarskolan på Fogelstad – som idé, text och historia.* Eds. Ebba Witt Brattström & Lena Lennerhed (2003).

7. *Moderaterna, marknaden och makten – svensk högerpolitik under avregleringens tid, 1976–1991.* Torbjörn Nilsson (2003).

8. *Upprorets estetik. Vittnesseminarier om kulturens politisering under 1960- och 1970-talet.* Ed. Lena Lennerhed (2005).

9. *Revolution på svenska – ett vittnesseminarium om jämställdhetens institutionalisering, politisering och expansion 1972–1976.* Ed. Anja Hirdman (2005).

10. *En högskola av ny typ? Två seminarier kring Södertörns högskolas tillkomst och utveckling.* Eds. Mari Gerdin & Kjell Östberg (2006).

11. *Hur rysk är den svenska kommunismen? Fyra bidrag om kommunism, nationalism och etnicitet.* Eds. Mari Gerdin & Kjell Östberg (2006).

12. *Ropen skalla – daghem åt alla! Vittnesseminarium om daghemskampen på 70-talet.* Eds. Mari Gerdin & Kajsa Ohrlander (2007).

13. *Makten i kanslihuset. Vittnesseminarium 16 maj 2006.* Eds. Emma Isaksson & Torbjörn Nilsson (2007).

14. *Partnerskapslagen – ett vittnesseminarium om partnerskapslagens tillkomst.* Eds. Emma Isaksson & Lena Lennerhed (2007).

15. *Vägar till makten – statsrådens och statssekreterarnas karriärvägar.* Anders Ivarsson Westerberg & Cajsa Niemann (2007).

16. *Sverige och Baltikums frigörelse. Två vittnesseminarier om storpolitik kring Östersjön 1991–1994.* Eds. Thomas Lundén & Torbjörn Nilsson (2008).

17. *Makten och trafiken i Stadshuset. Två vittnesseminarier om Stockholms kommunalpolitik.* Ed. Torbjörn Nilsson (2009).

18. *Norden runt i tvåhundra år. Jämförande studier om liberalism, konservatism och historiska myter.* Torbjörn Nilsson (2010).

19. *1989 med svenska ögon. Vittnesseminarium om Östeuropas omvandling.* Eds. Torbjörn Nilsson & Thomas Lundén (2010).

20. *Statsminister Göran Persson i samtal med Erik Fichtelius (1996–2006).* Ed. Werner Schmidt (2011).

21. *Bortom rösträtten. Politik, kön och medborgarskap i Norden.* Eds. Lenita Freidenwall & Josefin Rönnbäck (2011).

22. *Borgerlig fyrklöver intog Rosenbad – regeringsskiftet 1991.* Eds. Torbjörn Nilsson & Anders Ivarsson Westerberg (2011).

23. *Rivstart för Sverige – Alliansen och maktskiftet 2006.* Eds. Fredrik Eriksson & Anders Ivarsson Westerberg (2012).

24. *Det började i Polen – Sverige och Solidaritet 1980–1981.* Ed. Fredrik Eriksson (2013).

25. *Förnyelse eller förfall? Svenska försvaret efter kalla kriget.* Ed. Fredrik Eriksson (2013).

26. *Staten och granskningssamhället.* Eds. Bengt Jacobsson & Anders Ivarsson Westerberg (2013).

27. *Almedalen – varför är vi här? Så skapades en politikens marknadsplats – Ett vittnesseminarium om Almedalsveckan som politisk arena.* Ed. Kjell Östberg (2013).

28. *Anarkosyndikalismens återkomst i Spanien. SACs samarbete med CNT under övergången från diktatur till demokrati.* Ed. Per Lindblom (2014).

29. *När blev vården marknad? Vittnesseminarium i Almedalen.* Ed. Kristina Abiala (2014).

30. *Brinner "förorten"? Om sociala konflikter i Botkyrka och Huddinge.* Ed. Kristina Abiala (2014).

31. *Sea of Identities: A Century of Baltic and East European Experiences with Nationality, Class, and Gender.* Ed. Norbert Götz (2014).

32. *När räntan gick i taket: Vittnesseminarium om valutakrisen 1992.* Ed. Cecilia Åse (2015).

33. *Nordiskt samarbete i kalla krigets kölvatten. Vittnesseminarium med Uffe Ellemann-Jensen, Mats Hellström och Pär Stenbäck.* Eds. Johan Strang & Norbert Götz (2016).

34. *Solidariteten med Chile 1973–1989.* Eds. Yulia Gradskova & Monica Quirico (2016).

35. *25 år av skolreformer – hur började det? Vittnesseminarium om skolans kommunalisering och friskolereformen.* Ed. Johanna Ringarp (2017).

36. *Levande campus: Utmaningar och möjligheter för Södertörns högskola i den nya regionala stadskärnan i Flemingsberg.* Eds. Johanna Ringarp & Håkan Forsell (2017).

37. *Utbildningsvetenskap: Vittnesseminarium om ett vetenskapsområdes uppkomst, utveckling och samtida utmaningar.* Eds. Anders Burman, Daniel Lövheim & Johanna Ringarp (2018).

38. *Pontus Hultén på Moderna Museet: Vittnesseminarium på Södertörns högskola, 26 april 2017.* Ed. Charlotte Bydler, Andreas Gedin & Johanna Ringarp (2018).

39. *AIDS i Sverige: Hivepidemin och rörelserna.* Eds. Kjell Östberg & Lena Lennerhed (2019).

40. *Romerna och skolplikten: Hot eller möjlighet?* Ed. Håkan Blomqvist (2020).

41. *Sweden in Solidarity, Museums in Exile: The Chilean Resistance Museum in Solidarity with Salvador. Allende and the International Art Exhibition for Palestine.* Ed. Charlotte Bydler (2022).

42. *Kamp mot droger: En bok om Förbundet mot droger.* Kjell Östberg (2019).

43. *North and South: European Social Democracy in the 1970s.* Eds. Alan Granadino, Carl Marklund & Johan Strang (2021).

44. *Recollections of Joining the EU: Iberian and Nordic Experiences.* Eds. Alan Granadino, Peter Stadius & Carl Marklund (2023).

45. *Visions of the Nordic Model in Northern and Southern Europe (1970s-1990s).* Eds. Alan Granadino, Andreas Mørkved Hellenes & Carl Marklund (2023).

SÖDERTÖRNS HÖGSKOLA | STOCKHOLM
sh.se

AARHUS UNIVERSITY

UNIVERSITY OF HELSINKI
CENS · CENTRE FOR NORDIC STUDIES

NOS-HS The joint committee for
Nordic research councils in the
humanities and social sciences